The neoconservative experiment is back
with a vicious tidal wave!
H.

TURNING POINT

Hanny Hilmy, Ph.D

TURNING POINT

MOVING BEYOND NEOCONSERVATISM

PHILIP DeMONT AND J. EUGENE LANG

Published in 1999 by Stoddart Publishing Co. Limited
34 Lesmill Road, Toronto, Canada M3B 2T6
180 Varick Street, 9th Floor, New York, New York 10014

Distributed in Canada by:
General Distribution Services Ltd.
325 Humber College Blvd., Toronto, Ontario M9W 7C3
Tel. (416) 213-1919   Fax (416) 213-1917
Email customer.service@ccmailgw.genpub.com

Distributed in the United States by:
General Distribution Services Inc.
85 River Rock Drive, Suite 202, Buffalo, New York 14207
Toll-free Tel. 1-800-805-1083   Toll-free Fax 1-800-481-6207
Email gdsinc@genpub.com

03   02   01   00   99   1   2   3   4   5

Canadian Cataloguing in Publication Data

DeMont, Philip R. (Philip Russell)
Turning point: moving beyond neoconservatism

Includes bibliographical references and index.
ISBN 0-7737-3222-5

1. Conservatism – Canada. 2. Canada – Politics and government – 1993–   .*
3. Canada – Social policy. 4. Economics. I. Lang, J. Eugene. II. Title.

JC573.2.C3D45 1999   320.52'0971   C99-931461-0

Cover design: Angel Guerra
Text design: Tannice Goddard

THE CANADA COUNCIL | LE CONSEIL DES ARTS
FOR THE ARTS | DU CANADA
SINCE 1957 | DEPUIS 1957

*We acknowledge for their financial support of our publishing
program the Canada Council, the Ontario Arts Council, and
the Government of Canada through the Book Publishing
Industry Development Program (BPIDP).*

Printed and bound in Canada

To the brightest stars
in my small universe,
Heather, James, and Alanna
— PHILIP DEMONT

To my mother and father,
Jacqueline Lang and Eugene Lang Sr.
— J. EUGENE LANG

CONTENTS

PREFACE

The young public relations specialist paused over her lunch at a downtown Indian restaurant. She was answering the question, What would you consider to be an ideal political campaign?

"I suppose it would be one in which all the policy platforms are tacked to a bulletin board, leaving me to decide which one made the most sense."

That sentiment is a thread among many voters across the country. People are interested in weighing the promises and potential of political parties before marking their ballot. Why, then, are today's political battles fought so far from the policy front?

Too often public relations gimmicks take the place of a measured assessment of party platforms. Jamming phone-in shows with partisan callers and the spectacle of political leaders shouting at each other during televised debates — all this is supposed to pass for reasoned debate.

Policy discussions are left as an afterthought, to be introduced quickly and then abandoned.

That is the legacy of the past fifteen years of conservative ideas among political parties, the media, and think-tanks. After peaking in the late 1980s, neoconservatives have fallen into disarray, ironically resembling the exhausted liberals in the early part of that decade. These right-wing thinkers who once prided themselves on their debating skills now wield petty gamesmanship as their sword and public hectoring as their shield.

A policy vacuum has opened up in Canada and, to some extent, the United States. But even as the conservative era is drawing to a close, no liberal idea types have stepped forward to fill this vacuum with policies to push Canada ahead. Economic problems, such as high unemployment and income inequality, still exist. But neither the left nor the right has new ideas with which to attack them. Instead, both sides engage in ideological name-calling or simplistic solutions with little relevance to ordinary Canadians.

In this political world, economics takes a back seat. In past decades, great minds argued important issues. Nowadays, public policy types resemble ancient religious philosophers who spent their time estimating the number of angels that could fit on the head of a pin.

This book is our attempt to bring this debate back to a useful reality. The fact is, the popularity of government spending cuts, radical tax reductions, and the excessive elimination of business restrictions is declining. We ask the questions, How is this change in sentiment explainable in terms of economic policy? Why did this conservative streak appear in Canada and why is it receding? We also offer some ideas to fill the policy void. We do not present these ideas as tablets from the Mount. Instead, we put forward our modest suggestions believing that an obvious target is more likely to draw response from thinkers who for too long have kept their heads below the parapets. Only then will a real debate begin about what Canadians want and what Canada will look like in the next century.

As novice authors, we have relied heavily upon the talents of many people to get this volume published. We wish to thank all the people at Stoddart Publishing, especially Jack Stoddart and Don Bastian, whose comments and encouragement kept us on course. We also wish to thank Gerald Owen, whose judicious editing and sage insights helped sharpen the book's logic and style.

We are, of course, solely to blame for any remaining errors.

Philip DeMont
J. Eugene Lang
August 1999

INTRODUCTION
GROPING TOWARDS
THE NEW LIBERALISM

THE FAILURE OF ECONOMICS
AS PUBLIC POLICY

This is an age of political distrust and cynicism. Elected officials
are often viewed as unprincipled and undisciplined, relying upon catch-
phrases and five-second sound bites, not reasonable policy positions, to
snare voters.

Of course, other eras have faced a similar world-weariness among
electorates. This time, however, the world is heading into uncharted
waters. Countries face an unprecedented technological explosion, one
that threatens to swamp the capacity of governments to set rules and
the ability of the public to comprehend the extent of these changes.
People are bombarded with so much information, through the airwaves
and across fibre optic cables in the ground, that they have real difficulty
discerning measured debate from unstructured ranting. It seems that
anybody with a loud voice and a sufficiently offensive manner can get

1

on a talk show or secure a regular slot on a television panel.

Worst of all, there is a lingering pessimism, which, though lessening in recent years, still hangs over the public debate like an overcast sky in Newfoundland. Much of this gloom stems from the past twenty years, in which full-time jobs have become fewer in number, well-educated children have gone back to live with their parents, and the idea of a better life seems a quaint notion from our fathers' time. People see themselves as having few allies, whether among elected officials or businessmen. As a result, they are more interested in looking out for number one than in the past.

Few, if any, public policy analysts would have predicted such an outcome from the past fifteen years or so. The appearance of Ronald Reagan in the United States, Margaret Thatcher in the United Kingdom, and, to a lesser degree, Brian Mulroney in Canada was supposed to herald a new sunrise among Western nations. These leaders were going to return free markets and entrepreneurial achievement to the economic forefront. George Bush tried to entice people to give back to their communities through voluntarism instead of relying upon the heavy hand of government to help the less fortunate.

In some cases, taxes were cut. In others, government spending, usually seen as the reason for the higher levies in the first place, was chopped or at least capped. Most countries in Europe and North and South America were interested in removing government-created barriers to economic markets and, hence, potential growth. And more people did get involved in assisting their communities. The financial stagnation attributed to past liberal regimes was over, so the apologists claimed. In its place was a rugged capitalism, one that eliminated past excesses and relied upon individual abilities rather than public programs to drive an expanding economy.

A couple of decades later, however, the crankiness that afflicted voters at the end of the presidency of Jimmy Carter and during the last years of the reign of Pierre Trudeau has returned. Most politicians are once again viewed as cheats, liars, or, at best, mere incompetents. Consumers believe businesses are picking their pockets with complex products and services priced in a multitude of hard-to-understand ways. People publicly complaining about their economic lot are immediately labelled as part of a "special interest" and held up to scorn.

When this malaise occurred during the era of liberal-leaning governments, crabby voters turned to conservative political parties for solutions. So much so that, by the 1990s, deficit reduction and deregulation became the order of the day, with a smattering of privatization and social reform thrown in for good measure. Balanced budgets were expected of many governments. Appealing to the beleaguered middle class rather than cobbling together a disparate coalition of voters became the main winning political strategy.

That era has ended, however, with conservative leaders being replaced around the world by a new wave of non-ideological liberals. These men and women are pursuing solutions to existing problems, not causing new ones through doctrinaire efforts to push some kind of "etched-in-stone" social or economic agenda.

In part, conservatives lost their grip on power because they had reached the effective limits of their policies. Unemployment remained high in historical terms in most countries, except the U.S., even after a large dose of market reform. National economies started growing faster. But the distribution of these gains among various income classes and geographical regions remained uneven. And the pay packets of many workers, especially those in blue-collar trades, were not growing.

This time around, conservatives had little new to offer. They could only promise more of the same: reducing union power and cutting more jobs and wages. And this appeal had begun to fall on deaf ears.

Even in Ontario, where the Conservatives of Mike Harris were re-elected in 1999, the poor campaign by his Liberal Party challengers rather than his party's own appeal appeared to be the key to victory.

THE RETURN OF THE LIBERALS

The new-style liberals, however, do not present many fresh answers of their own to their countries' economic and social woes. They have a more positive vision of where their nations are headed, but not a clearer road map with which to make the journey. Rhetoric has replaced policy as the main lever for many voters. U.S. President Bill Clinton and British Prime Minister Tony Blair epitomize the new crowd, always ready to talk about lending a helping hand, but only within the context of a balanced budget. Clinton, Blair, and their lesser political brothers, such as Canada's Jean Chrétien, have not discovered a new industrial or monetary policy to solve current economic woes.

The U.S. still suffers from an unequal income distribution and a poor division of the spoils of its recent boom. Canada faces a high jobless rate, especially by national historical standards. And Britain is heading into a period of minimal growth.

What has changed, and what helped markedly in bringing these liberals to power, are the terms that they use to describe the challenges and opportunities of their countries. Blair talks about his "third way," between utopian socialism (a real threat in the U.K.'s case) and Thatcher's harsh style of capitalism. Clinton does not have a media-friendly term for his mixture of helping the less well-off and encouraging the remarkable American entrepreneurial spirit.

In 1993, Canadians contrasted Progressive Conservative leader Kim Campbell's dour talk about the need to accept diminished expectations with Chrétien's sunny images of "cranes in the sky" and picked the latter by an overwhelming majority.

In this decade, voters in most countries have grown tired of their politicians setting cramped limits to public policy, telling them that all they can expect is whatever hand they are dealt, good or bad, by the impersonal marketplace. The voters want more, and generally it has been the liberal politicians who have been willing to push the bounds of the people's psyche. In the past their fine words would have merely been caramel-smooth banter in the service of placating any and all voting groups. These days, however, the rhetoric represents a different type of leadership, an ability to move people beyond their limited realities into a land of imagination, of "why not" instead of "why try." After years of reduced goals, people appear once again ready to demand that their governments raise the ceilings heretofore constricting their countries.

FOG AS A VIRTUE

This is an era when figuring out how to connect a telephone call faster is more important than leading men into battle. Radicals sport two-piece suits and talk about the Internet. Swift change no longer comes from the barrel of a gun or rides in on a tank. Instead, the new guerrillas are computer geeks, or at least talk like them; they have some understanding of how technology affects the modern economy and know how to tap into society's concern for those less well-off while recognizing the importance of free markets.

In a world where the lines between politicians and businessmen, left and right, and economic and social policy have blurred beyond recognition, leaders like Clinton and Blair fit like a glove. Soaring rhetoric and clever packaging, not policy, are their weapons. They can inspire and move people without actually promising much that is concrete.

Using hard-to-define beliefs is not so much election strategy as a necessity. Past leaders had terrific enemies with whom to grapple, be they Soviet toughs or fascist demigods. The wars between ideologies, however, ended with the crumbling of the Berlin Wall, leaving the implementation of roughly similar plans as the great proving ground for new presidents and prime ministers. These days, political debates resemble tiffs between overly excited bureaucrats rather than struggles between competing visionaries. The winner is usually the person who can convince voters of the greater viability of his or her plan for navigating the same public policy river.

The question is not which tributary to take but how to keep the raft afloat during the journey.

Because of the lack of ideology and the excess of yapping, some accuse Blair, Clinton, and their kind of hugging the centre stripe of the political highway a little too closely. They are not men of conviction but of compromise, ready to sell their soul for a deal, reads the indictment.

That very flexibility, however, is their biggest strength. Instead of wasting time and energy seeking out doctrinaire differences few would believe in, the new liberals look for the best way to cross the ever-shrinking divide between left and right to push the government's agenda forward.

The ideological differences between liberals and conservatives are less substantial than at any time since the late 1950s. In this world, leaders who are eager to overthrow the few remaining Communist leaders or reinstate conservative social mores look like throwbacks to an era when civil rights marchers were accused of being "fellow-travellers" and the bullwhip was held to be a legitimate expression of states' rights.

In fact, neoconservatives are now out of fashion because the popularity of their economic program extended only as far as balancing the budget and maybe cutting taxes. Their social agenda appears pretty much dead.

What drove voters to embrace the right wing in the first place was the worry that governments would be unable to meet repayment schedules, and that countries would go into receivership. Voters wanted someone who could talk tough, balance the books, and get the fiscal house in shape. But as the 1990s end, budgets are pretty well balanced and most economies are in better shape than at the beginning of the decade. Many people have lost their ill-tempered edge. They are unenthusiastic about pursuing further cutbacks to essential services, like health care and education, that could affect their neighbours and themselves.

Clinton and Blair rode this inevitable liberal swing in voter sentiment to electoral victories. But they also captured the mood of their country-men through an adroit combination of inspiring chat and fresh style.

While often accused of using pollsters to set policy, in reality politi-cal victors usually do more than discern which underlying trends to exploit. They also amplify and direct the way voters are headed. Maybe they cannot fundamentally change the path upon which the feet of the electorate are set. But they certainly can dictate the speed and what stops are made along the way.

CANADA'S TIME

Up here, the political shift to the centre is less striking. But the country's conservative movement is seriously wounded.

Reform Party leader Preston Manning, the man most responsible for getting right-wing ideas on Canada's political agenda, has twice failed to crack Ontario in federal elections. While his party gained votes and seats overall in 1993 and 1997, Manning has no members east of the Manitoba-Ontario border.

Worse, Reform's current popularity is still the same as it was six years ago. And a large chunk of the Progressive Conservative vote could move to the Liberals if Manning headed up a united Reform-Tory party, according to at least one national pollster.[1]

Provincially, there is little trace of the U.S.-style rhetoric and hard-edged policies that appeared ready to sweep regional capitals four years ago. In British Columbia, NDP Premier Glen Clark, a genuinely unlikeable leader, managed to hold on to power in the 1996 election, beating the seemingly sure winner and closet conservative Gordon Campbell, a man with all the style of an old-fashioned dime-store Indian statue.

In 1995, Ontario's Mike Harris, under the flag of his Common Sense Revolution, led his Conservative Party to a big electoral victory. Back then, he talked tough about getting people off welfare by cutting benefits and instituting mandatory work programs. Harris also promised to get government off the backs of the middle class and small business, themes that resonated with disgruntled voters in Canada's largest province.

During the 1999 provincial campaign, however, Harris changed his tune significantly. Instead of using hard-nosed rhetoric to promote conservative issues, the Ontario premier talked about the need to protect health care and improve education. He even founded some conservation areas just before calling the June 3 vote, a grudging move to improve his government's image on the environment.

To be sure, in the latest campaign, Harris still nodded towards the Tory's traditional core with, for instance, policies to force welfare recipients to take drug tests. But the possibility of introducing private hospital and medical coverage and the idea of voucher public schools, in which parents could chose among different taxpayer-funded institutions, were not found in the Tory platform.

Harris genuflected towards his conservative core vote by offering a second tax cut, this time reducing personal income tax rates by 20 percent and the provincial portion of the property tax also by 20 percent, and then headed back to the political middle with new spending programs. His majority victory indicated more a lack of believable alternatives than an overwhelming endorsement of his government.

In Alberta, Ralph Klein, whose election in 1992 set off the conservative tsunami among provincial governments, still spends time on issues that get right-wingers worked up, such as gay rights and legalized gambling, but not in ways the right-wingers want. Instead of introducing laws to restrict rights based upon sexual orientation, Klein let stand a human rights tribunal ruling that gives gays protected legal status. He has refused to use the notwithstanding clause in the Canadian constitution to override that decision. In 1998, Klein allowed communities across the province to hold referendums on whether they wanted video lottery machines in their towns and cities. Most areas voted in favour of this high-tech banditry, harpooning another conservative position, this time a religious one, against games of chance.

Of course, Klein is not in danger of losing his job any time soon. Conservatives have run this province since 1971, when Peter Lougheed beat the Social Credit Party. Even with his strong electoral position, however, Klein appears uninterested in pushing the conservative agenda any further. Like his counterparts in other provinces, he has discovered the political centre and appears ready to occupy it.

The western provinces are not the only areas experiencing an ideological sea change. Out east, the story is actually the same. Even though three of the provinces are led by Tories, all are of the distinctly red variety. In the summer of 1999, John Hamm and Bernard Lord led their parties to victory. In both cases, voter fatigue with the province's governing Liberals was the crucial factor. In Prince Edward Island, Pat Binns looks and sounds like his Liberal Maritime colleagues.

VACUUM

Even as conservatives retreat across Canada, however, the Liberals in Ottawa have been unable to build on their opponents' weakness to present a vision of where the country should be headed. In the capital, confusion, not confidence, has greeted this moderate turn in national politics.

Chrétien has won two back-to-back majorities and led the country for six years. Yet, his government has failed to establish an economic policy that might move the country beyond successfully balancing the national budget. Chrétien has relied upon Paul Martin, the finance minister, to set the government's economic agenda and wrestle the federal budget deficit to the ground. Here, Martin succeeded, eliminating the federal shortfall of $42 billion and presenting the first balanced budget in Ottawa in twenty-eight years.

The problem is what to do next. In 1962, the New York Yankee slugger Roger Maris smacked 33 home runs, placing him fifth in the American League in this category. Yet even hometown New York fans booed him. The previous season, Maris had belted what was then a major league record of 61 four-baggers. And the Bronx faithful, never Maris boosters at the best of times, were decidedly unhappy with next year's performance. Ottawa is in the same position. Having stamped out the deficit, the government faces greater pressure from the financial community to assault Canada's high tax rates and its mountain of $650 billion in debt. Even in the face of the present economic expansion, however, the country's unemployment rate hovers between 7 and 8 percent. So, the government has its traditional "spend and tax" constituencies pushing the administration to boost job-creation efforts. Meanwhile, some middle- and upper-income Canadians are pining wistfully for any kind of tax cut.

So far, Martin has responded in true Canadian fashion, offering a bit of something for everyone. In the 1999 budget, he cut income taxes marginally. He also increased spending on traditional programs such as health care. The Liberal government has tinkered with its own version of an industrial strategy. The point person is the industry minister John Manley, who has preached the gospel of the information highway, pursuing the vision of an Internet port in every house. Ottawa is also musing about tackling Canada's overall productivity problem but is not sure of its strategy.

In each case, Ottawa has pushed its economic agenda with all the enthusiasm of a scotch drinker at a temperance society meeting. Every item is getting just enough money or attention from Ottawa to stay alive but not enough to be pursued effectively. Many political analysts argue that these Liberal tactics should come as no surprise. Learning from his predecessors, Chrétien's economic platform resembles a church supper: something for everyone, but none of it particularly tasty.

That reasoning is too shallow to explain why, in spite of a conservative retreat, Liberals in Ottawa and many in other countries have been singularly unable to articulate a coherent economic strategy. Electoral considerations are not all that matters in constructing policy and programs. In fact, these governments are offering a buffet of programs because they have very few ways to battle the day's major economic problems: growth and unemployment.

SHOOT THE ECONOMIST

In essence, it is the academics, not the politicians, who have failed Canadians.

Decades ago, federal parties differed on budgetary and employment policy because they followed divergent economic theories. Generally, Liberals and social democrats used the thinking of John Maynard Keynes, promoting the use of budget deficits and tax policy to produce new jobs or cool down inflation. Conservatives, on the other hand, placed their faith in Adam Smith's invisible hand of the marketplace, as well as Milton Friedman's monetarist doctrine, to create prosperity.

During the past thirty years, public policy economics has undergone fundamental changes. Where once Keynesians ruled the roost, monetarists took command, harpooning the prevailing orthodoxy with some clever theoretical manipulations. This group, however, only held sway among intellectuals for a few years as rapid changes to the underlying monetary measures made their systems unworkable.

Then, along came the most effective bomb throwers of all: the rational expectationists. Bizarre seeming at first blush, this theory of how quickly people react to economic change essentially put the final nail in the coffin of the crude Keynesianism practised in the '50s and '60s.

But it also sealed the fate of strict monetarism and other less credible theories, such as supply-side economics. In short, rational expectations — the theory that people act reasonably most times and markets clear in short order — killed everything in the academic economic world. All of a sudden, many long-standing theories about how the economy works lacked a sound philosophical base from which to make useful prescriptions to government.

The importance of the theory was not in how politicians reacted, but how economists did. The academic crowd that usually could be counted upon to help elected officials to devise better policies were too busy in their university bunkers devising ways to save their pet theories from the new onslaught. In the 1990s, politicians have been left to fend for themselves in the area of economic policy. And they are stumbling ahead, picking policies that might appease voters, with little regard for their overall economic consequences.

MUDDLING THROUGH

This type of "no theory" governing has been practised in Western economies for more than a decade. Governments are at a loss about how to approach economic policy-making.

As a result, ideology was turned on its head in the 1980s. A Conservative government in Ottawa ran up the largest budget deficits in Canadian history. The usually profligate Liberals then got credit for putting the country's finances on a more solid footing in this decade.

In the United States, Reagan's right-wing administration produced the largest budgetary shortfalls in that country's history, making the former movie actor the last great Keynesian. Then Bill Clinton, the most charismatic conservative-liberal since John F. Kennedy, attacked government spending and eliminated the U.S. deficit.

The reason for this counter-intuitive policy-making by liberals and conservatives is not that the new policies of these governments were much more politically saleable than the old ones of previous administrations. It is simply that very little in the economic world makes sense any more.

Governments have been willing to do the little bits that they knew would generate positive headlines in newspapers even if they failed to produce much economic response. A small tax cut is trumpeted as the next great idea. Liberal administrations pursue conservative policies and Conservatives push liberal ideas, in the hope of gaining a few more votes and, almost incidentally, helping the economy.

A BEAM OF LIGHT

Finally, as the decade — and the twentieth century — grinds to a close, a pair of academics have devised theories that, when used in combination, give governments a way out of the black hole.

Paul Romer, a professor at Stanford University in California, has made a career of explaining a part of the economy that most analysts leave alone, namely the sources of growth and innovation. Conventional economic models manipulate the level of economic demand and the supply of factors of production like labour. But the level of technical prowess is assumed to be a given and not subject to changes by economic policy.

Romer thinks this assumption silly and, instead, figures that economies can "learn to learn" by investing in research and allowing private enterprise more of a say in what developments will be pursued in publicly funded education.

He also believes that the information economy exhibits increasing returns to scale, which means the bigger you are, the bigger you will get. Traditional economic theory says, as you add more machines, the company reaches its optimal size, beyond which the additional machinery reduces the firm's profits and efficiency.

Not so in Romer's world. In the new high-tech age, firms that get access first to new data can absorb this information in ever-increasing amounts, giving these corporations a growing advantage over lagging competitors.

Romer's thinking offers a role for the government of a smaller nation, such as Canada. Ottawa can take a leading hand in developing information technology infrastructure and policies to assist Canadian high-tech firms to catch up to — or at least prevent falling further behind — their ever-growing competitors in the U.S. and in Europe.

REICH

If Romer's work offers a rationale for government action in the areas of tax policy and infrastructure, the ideas of Robert Reich, the diminutive former U.S. Secretary of Labor, give public policy purpose in enhancing important social assets such as education and health care.

Reich believes large global companies are in the process of dividing their production and design functions among different countries and locations. In the past, firms needed to maintain their head offices close to their plants because of the importance of exchanging information between facilities, and so that management could keep an eye on the entire operation.

In this decade, however, advances in communications technology and management techniques have lessened the need to locate facilities in one area or country. Instead, firms like General Motors Corp. locate various parts of their worldwide operations in different regions: Canada, the United States, Latin America, and Asia.

Governments often try to halt this inexorable decentralizing trend by waving tax breaks or other incentives in front of the companies to entice them to place their manufacturing or production wings in their jurisdictions. Reich views the loss of power by central governments as inevitable and, hence, such activity as futile. Administrations need to figure out better ways to improve their economies.

Manufacturing jobs, which many nations treasured during the industrial age, are less important in post-industrial society. Instead, the seemingly sterile manipulation of data signals is now the key to the shape of the modern economy. Fighting for software, high-tech, and service jobs makes sense; battling to keep older-style employment banging out plastic toys does not.

Besides, quickly industrializing nations, such as Vietnam and Indonesia, have teeming cities full of eager workers who are willing to accept a wage the fraction of a Western employee's, to do the same low-skilled work. So North American and European governments should work to attract value-added, higher-wage jobs in areas like computer software design and sophisticated production. The strategy seems to be: Do not fight to make baubles and trinkets. Instead, strive for the work designing these bits of plastic.

Reich's thinking leads to the conclusion that governments should implement policies to develop the most sophisticated workforce possible. As well, his ideas highlight social programs as important tools to improve the quality of a nation's employees. Chopping away at hospitals, schools, and the welfare system means a poorer quality workforce with less chance of finding long-term meaningful employment, and a consequent drag on the country's productivity. Without a base of educated, healthy workers, the prospect of attracting sophisticated work, about which thinkers like the Canadian technology guru Don Tapscot and his U.S. counterpart George Gilder talk, becomes almost impossible.

WHERE THIS BOOK IS HEADING

Turning Point traces the rise and fall of neoconservative political economy in this country and offers a liberal battle plan for Ottawa and the provinces to use in developing an economy for the twenty-first century. The widespread dismantling of the welfare state, the movement for large tax cuts, and the focus on debt reduction have all reached their zenith and are receding. Romer and Reich give the coming wave of liberal governments a theory upon which to design programs to create jobs and increase prosperity across a wide swatch of the country.

In this book we trace the roots of Canada's conservative revival from Preston Manning's Reform Party and its influence on Ottawa through governments in Ontario and Alberta. We also examine the policy jam in which these two Tory provincial administrations find themselves and why Manning will never become Canada's prime minister.

In addition, we outline the part that economic theory played in the rise of the conservative movement and in its ultimate failure. Finally, with the help of Reich and Romer, we lay out the threads of a policy to assist administrations in designing a more modern economy.

In the end, the current wave of conservative economic thinking, maybe necessary in a time when many believed in the omnipotence of government, is at an end. These theorizers can take society no farther in their present incarnation.

But there is a policy vacuum in Ottawa. The federal government is seemingly unwilling to lead Canada to the next economic level. Following Romer and Reich could bring this country into a new era, end the sterile debates about continuing deep social and tax cuts, and finally get Canadians thinking about the real issues for developing an information age economy.

ONE
THE LONG MARCH
OF THE NEOCONS

In the United States it is called neoconservatism. In Europe it is referred to as neoliberalism and the British often call it the new right. And in Canada, perhaps fittingly, all these terms mean the same thing and are interchangeable, although, in typical two-solitudes fashion, French Canadians seem to favour neoliberalism whereas English Canadians use neoconservatism. Beginning with the election of Margaret Thatcher's government in Britain in 1979, conservative political parties have arisen and gained power in many countries of the industrialized world. Different nations tried this new right experiment at various strengths, with Thatcher being the guiding light. Canadians latched on to a weaker variation of this conservative form. Diluted as it was, Canada's resurgent right wing was a potent tonic for the country's economic ailments.

HOW DO WE GO BACK IN TIME
TO ADVANCE THE FUTURE?

In fact there is not much that is new with these modern conservatives; the new right is rooted in the old classical ideas of promoting and preserving traditional thinking and values, both in the economic and social spheres.[1] That sounds reasonable, except that the ideology has some glaring contradictions. On the one hand, neoconservatives want small government, of a kind that removes itself from the marketplace. But at the same time they favour an administration that is vigorous in advancing certain social policies and is not shy about using the law to push this agenda. The new right wants it both ways: the evisceration of the welfare state and a sharply reduced role for government in the economy at the same time as expanded public dabbling through toughness on crime, restrictions or outright prohibitions on abortion, tight immigration policies, and some religious-based laws, particularly in the area of sexual orientation. They also generally oppose measures designed to deal with race or sexual discrimination, such as affirmative action or employment equity legislation.

While the economic side of the neoconservative agenda has some legs, the social aspect has not really made its mark anywhere outside the United States. In the land of the free and home of the brave, the religious right has enjoyed more influence than in Canada or Europe. Nevertheless, there is no real future for this kind of puritanical social agenda in the modern world. Europeans, Canadians, and Americans still want their sex, drugs, and rock and roll. And this is especially true of the large and powerful baby boomer generation. Maybe they are not interested in extending the rights of certain groups, but they have shown little interest in reviving such fine policies as anti-buggery laws.

Even in the U.S., there are practical limits to social conservatism, a movement that has recently exercised considerable influence over the Republican Party, but in the process has alienated middle-of-the-road voters and hamstrung the party's electoral chances, most notably in the 1996 presidential election. In the United States, social conservatives were at the apex of their power that year and have since receded in significance, partly as a result of their front-and-centre involvement in the crusade to remove Bill Clinton from office because of his sexual indiscretions. That effort did little more than annoy the vast majority of Americans, who did not support Clinton's ouster, largely because he has presided over a period of profound economic prosperity, which is what really counts for American voters (as his adviser James Carville famously pointed out in the 1992 presidential campaign, "It's the economy, stupid," that matters).

Economic neoconservatism, rooted in classical economics (i.e., the economics espoused by thinkers like Adam Smith and Alfred Marshall), is a different matter. This side of the conservative coin has enjoyed considerable success over the past twenty years in Britain, the U.S., New Zealand, and Canada, to name a few salient examples. Before it began to influence political parties and governments, conservative economics was promoted by a herd of British and American academics, the most notable of whom are F.A. Hayek and Milton Friedman, authors of the celebrated conservative bibles *A Road to Serfdom* and *Capitalism and Freedom*. Friedman and Hayek are fierce advocates of the classical economic virtues of free markets, unhindered trade, fiscal prudence, price stability, low taxes, and a much reduced role for the state compared to the one that prevailed in the post-war period.

Of course there was also Arthur Laffer, the favourite economist of the Reagan administration and ostensible founder of "supply-side" economics, a loony school of thought that argued governments could actually increase revenues by cutting taxes, thus giving a rationale for such a policy even in the face of large deficits. Laffer, however, unlike Hayek and Friedman, was never taken seriously by the economics profession. And since Reagan's tax cuts contributed to the ballooning of the U.S. deficit, Laffer's ideas have faded into obscurity even within the neocon movement. Still, prominent journalists and commentators in the U.S., such as William Kristol, William F. Buckley Jr., and William Bennett, and in Canada, like David Frum, William Watson, Terence Corcoran, and other writers for Conrad Black's *National Post*, have been leading standard-bearers of neoconservative economics, some even resurrecting Laffer's failed theory.

As their main strength, economic neocons have a well-defined policy agenda that is a reaction to the perceived failures of big government. Their thinking is based on the alleged merits of a smaller state — particularly smaller central government — principally through cutting the size of the welfare state, which, they argue, breeds inefficiency and laziness. To the new right mind, the welfare state is the major cause of deficits and debt (and unemployment for that matter), while other government expenses, such as defence, which neoconservatives generally want to increase, are minimized as sources of the budget problem. To get to the promised land of a smaller state, neocons favour balancing budgets and enacting legislation etching the principle of fiscal rectitude in stone; privatization of state enterprises and contracting-out of public services; reducing government rules and regulations that affect business; decentralized government; free trade; and price stability.

In Canada this "old as new" thinking found voice in the 1980s and 1990s through interest groups like the Business Council on National Issues and think-tanks like the Fraser and C. D. Howe Institutes. More importantly, various provincial party leaders, such as Ontario's Mike

Harris, Alberta's Ralph Klein, and B.C.'s Gordon Campbell, have carried the free market economic banner to the wider public. However, organized neoconservatism in Canada really begins with the creation of the Reform Party, led by Preston Manning, son of the long-serving Social Credit premier of Alberta, Ernest Manning.

In the 1980s, many critics held up the government of Brian Mulroney as Canada's first neoconservative regime. That view does not stand up to scrutiny. To be sure, some powerful elements of the Mulroney government wanted to jump on the Reagan bandwagon and the prime minister himself had great personal hopes of affinity with the global new right icons of his era, namely Thatcher and Reagan. Mulroney's governments, however, did not deliver a straight right program to Canadians. The Progressive Conservatives had some economic policies that went further down the road to freeing up the market than those of their predecessors. The most significant examples are the Canada-U.S. Free Trade Agreement, the ending of universality in some social programs, such as old age security and family allowances, privatization of a few Crown corporations like Air Canada, and unqualified support for the Bank of Canada's policy of price stability. This last continued even in the face of sharply declining public support for the Tories, which was partly attributable to the Bank's high interest rate policy.

On the social and economic fronts, however, the Mulroney government was responsible for many initiatives that were anathema to neocons, like the liberalization of the country's immigration and criminal justice policies, the establishment of regional development agencies to hand out government cash, and back-handed tax increases like the de-indexation of personal income tax brackets and credits and the establishment of so-called high income surtaxes.[2] Mulroney's Conservatives were also perhaps Canada's last fiscally profligate federal government, running among the largest deficits both in the aggregate and as a percentage of GDP in Canadian history. Such fiscal shortfalls were the norm under Mulroney even during periods of strong growth, culminating in the infamous $42 billion deficit of 1992-93. These are not the makings of a proud neocon legacy.

PRESTON MANNING AND THE REFORM PARTY: PIONEERS IN THE WILDERNESS

Neoconservatism at the federal level in Canada begins with Manning and the Reform Party. To most political observers this is a self-evident and non-controversial statement, but if we are to believe Tom Flanagan, a former Reform chief policy guru, Manning is not a right-winger at all but rather holds eclectic views that range across the ideological spectrum. Flanagan claims that Manning's ideology cannot really be pinned down because he eschews the label "conservative" and draws inspiration and guidance from his deeply held evangelical Christian beliefs and a variety of intellectual traditions and individuals, including the Czech president, writer, and former dissident Vaclav Havel.[3] Flanagan's characterization of the private Manning may be accurate, but to anyone who has followed Manning's career, especially during his years as MP for Calgary South-West, it is clear that his public persona is firmly in the neoconservative tradition. And it is the public Manning that counts when trying to establish his influence on Canadian politics.

There can also be little serious argument that the Reform Party, including both its MPs and core voting group, is neoconservative at least in the economic sphere and probably in the social domain as well. Certainly Flanagan does not argue this; indeed one of his chief criticisms of Manning is that he is not conservative enough to satisfy the Reform rank and file and intellectuals like himself and the former MP Stephen Harper, both of whom have left their positions in the party due to conflicts with Manning over the ideologically impure direction in which they claim he is taking Reform.

For the most part, Reformers represent the former right wing of the federal Tory party who had become disillusioned with the centrism of the Mulroney government and, in particular, its failures to reduce the budget deficit and cut taxes. The Mulroney fiscal legacy remains lamentable for many die-hard Tories who saw their party electorally decimated in 1993 and barely resuscitated in 1997, due to Reform's presence, which drained off the Tory's conservative support. This new right-wing army also absorbed voters who previously belonged to ultra-conservative parties such as Social Credit, Confederation of Regions, and Christian Heritage.[4] Recent initiatives to unite the country's conservative parties, largely spearheaded by Manning and the Reform Party, are an attempt to integrate the fragmented neocon movement. Ironically, in this effort to create a "united alternative" party that might defeat the Liberals and form a national government, neoconservatives may snuff out their own movement. Such a party, drawing in Reformers, Progressive Conservatives, and even some Liberals, will be a very broad church and not a pure right-wing party. To attract a broad range of support, the new party may be forced to jettison some conservative policies for the sake of electoral victory. Consequently, we are seeing some of Reform's harder-core MPs openly rejecting the united alternative concept and directly challenging Manning, partly on the ground that a new entity would water down Reform-style conservatism.

Such a compromise would be jarring. Many of the Reform MPs, including Manning himself, appear to be social conservatives and certainly elements of the party's platform are in this tradition, such as their tough victim-first criminal justice policies, opposition to state-run daycare, and desire to see churches and other charitable organizations supplant government as the major providers of social services.

However, Reform has tended to mute its social agenda, especially since the 1993 federal election, when the party began to believe it had a real chance to form a government some day. The tendency to downplay the social side of its policy ledger reflects a recognition on the part of the Reform leadership that this component of its agenda simply will not sell in Canada. Manning, and key strategists like Rick Anderson, a former Liberal backroom boy, seem to realize that, if the social conservatism of many Reform MPs leaks out in unvarnished form, it will likely kill the party's electoral chances, especially in moderate Ontario, where it must win big to have any chance of forming a national government.

The embarrassing episode in 1995 when the Reform MP Herb Grubel suggested during a House of Commons debate that successive governments had created a lazy, "spoiled-child" culture within "South Sea island" Native communities by giving in too easily to the financial demands of Aboriginal groups, exposed a side of Reform that won't sell in Canada and that can, and in this case did, produce a backlash. What was worse was that Grubel was no lunch-pail member of the Reform caucus speaking out of turn. He was in fact the most intellectual of their class of 1993 MPs, having been a leading academic economist and a key architect of and spokesperson for Reform's economic agenda.[5]

More bone-headed public statements embarrassed the party when Bob Ringma and Dave Chatters, two B.C. MPs, suggested that it is legitimate for small business owners to keep their visible minority or gay employees at the back of the store if this will improve business. These members were chastised by many in the party, but only lightly. Worse, Manning's expulsion at the same time of a moderate MP from Calgary, Jan Brown, signalled that the party was unwilling to tolerate different views, but willing to coddle bigots.

These episodes illustrated a stark and unattractive side of Reform social conservatism that Manning realizes he cannot afford to let surface again. Indeed, at the recent United Alternative conference, discussions of policy issues in general, but especially social policy, were eschewed by the Reform leadership for fear that a bigoted comment here or homophobic slur there would slip out in front of the cameras. This suppression of unpopular views was reflective of Manning's efforts to keep a lid on the social side of Reform and put the focus on their economics, which has proven to have electoral legs, and not just in the West.

REFORM ECONOMICS 101

When Reform was founded in the late 1980s, the Canadian economy was performing better than at any time in the previous twenty years. Shortly after the Mulroney government took office in 1984, the economy began to take off and, by the end of the decade, the unemployment rate had dropped to under 8 percent, as compared to the intolerably high 11.9 percent jobless level of 1983. During the early Mulroney years, however, Ottawa's deficit became a growing concern. The budget shortfall, supposedly to be run in bad economic times and be paid off in good ones, seemed to have developed an internal and unstoppable momentum, increasing even during the '80s boom, reaching $30 billion or so as 1990 approached. Federal governments had run deficits consistently since the late 1960s. But there was some counter-cyclical rationale for these shortfalls during the '70s and early '80s, mainly because the economy was in the doldrums. Mulroney's Tories presided over a relatively strong economy yet seemed unable, despite their tough fiscal rhetoric and some tangible efforts,[6] to contain deficit growth, let alone reduce it.

In 1987, the annual federal deficit stood at $30.6 billion, as high as the levels under the fiscally challenged Trudeau government. Deficits, however, were not yet really a big public issue during the late 1980s.

The economy during these years, at least on the surface, remained strong and the unemployment rate was low relative to the previous few years. In early 1989 a Gallup poll revealed that even though the federal deficit was close to $29 billion that year, only 31 percent of those surveyed were very concerned about such massive budgetary shortfalls.[7] These are the years when places like Toronto experienced vacancy rates approaching zero percent, real estate values shot up to new heights, and employment reached levels unheard-of for twenty years. We had stories of young people fresh out of university getting jobs in the overheated Toronto financial sector over the phone in a matter of hours. This was not a time of public angst over federal, or for that matter provincial, fiscal policy. The major public issues in the late '80s were free trade and, believe it or not, constitutional reform, not deficits and debt.

To his credit, Manning seemed to realize at this juncture that the deficit — and by implication the welfare state, the overall size of government, and tax levels — would become a huge issue for Canadians. By relentlessly pursuing the fiscal issue, which was totally consistent with Reform's economic philosophy, Manning walked into a political void created by the lack of real, focused attention to these issues by the established opposition parties and sitting governments. Manning thus became the pioneer in making government spending a major public issue, thereby putting neoconservative economics on the political map.

The Reform Party's economic mindset is evident in its 1990 policy document called *Principles and Policies.* For the first time in living memory here was a political party spelling out a clear neoconservative economic program, although such an agenda had not been electorally road-tested by any of the federal, or for that matter provincial, political parties. The policy manifesto was either a bold, self-confident, and perceptive move by Reform's leadership in anticipation of a rightward shift in Canadian politics, or a more short-sighted populist attempt to court conservative voters in Alberta who, by this point, were totally disillusioned with the Mulroney government's fiscal record and constitutional agenda. Either way its forward thinking established Reform as Canada's first federal new right political party.

The core of Reform's early economic agenda was a program of expenditure reduction to be achieved by cutting the federal bureaucracy, eliminating subsidies and tax concessions to business, and sharply reducing the welfare state. Under "Resolution One" of the manifesto, Reform also committed itself to enacting a law that would require the government to balance the budget in each three-year period or else call an election on the issue. The party also proposed the privatization of most federal Crown corporations, such as Petro-Canada (most of which was eventually sold off by the Mulroney government) and Canada Post.

On taxes, the party called for fundamental reform, leading to a "simple and visible system of taxation, including the possibility of a flat tax."[8] The replacement of Canada's progressive income tax system (in which people pay an increasing amount in taxes as they move up the income scale) by some form of flat tax, which Alberta's Ralph Klein floated in 1999, is often a long-term objective of neoconservatives. For Reform, however, to advocate this as early as 1990 was unusual. By way of comparison, in the United States, usually light-years ahead of Canada in its support of conservative economic policies, the flat income tax has yet to be advocated by any serious Republican presidential nominee, although it was the cornerstone of Steve Forbes's failed 1996 bid for the Republican nomination, as well as his run for the nomination in 2000.

Taxes aside, Canada's welfare state would come in for Reform's most radical surgery in the effort to both reduce the federal deficit and eliminate the alleged culture of dependency and sloth that resulted from these programs. For starters, any residual universality in income security benefits was to be eliminated (although the Tories had already achieved this by 1989 through their "clawbacks" of benefits if one's income was too high).[9] A Reform government would also actively "encourage families, communities, non-governmental organizations, and the private sector to reassume their duties and responsibilities in the social services area."[10] Ideally, remaining government benefits would be delivered through the income tax system, resulting in a so-called guaranteed annual income for Canadians. This approach to income support would replace a whole host of programs, including the Child Tax Credit, various personal exemptions, federal contributions to social assistance and retirement plans, social housing, and daycare deductions.

In this grab bag, Reform's most radical and important proposal is the guaranteed annual income, a notion that sounds liberal or even social-democratic. In fact this idea was spawned the conservative economist Milton Friedman. The belief here was that you could help the less well-off by giving them a payment through the income tax system, in effect a refund even without paying taxes. This approach would remove the need for a costly bureaucracy to administer social payments. Of course, the key here is the amount of income that is to be guaranteed, and on this critical point, Reform is, not surprisingly, silent. Suffice it to say that Manning, like Friedman, was likely envisioning a highly restricted guaranteed annual income program. As various studies have indicated over the years, the costs of a decent benefit kicking in at a reasonable income level would be enormous, making short-term deficit reduction, Reform's core objective, virtually impossible to attain.[11]

To round things out on the income security front, Reform advocated the immediate elimination of discriminatory unemployment insurance elements such as regional entrance requirements and regionally extended benefit phases. The party's main objective was to return UI to a pure insurance program and remove its social policy or redistributive elements.

In the domain of fiscal federalism, Reform again showed its classically conservative colours by advocating a more decentralized government, even though Canada already has one of the least dominant central governments on the globe. Under a Reform government, Ottawa would provide the provinces with unconditional transfers of sections of the tax base and would curtail the use of federal spending in areas of provincial jurisdiction, like health care and education.

THE POLITICS OF REFORM ECONOMICS

By the standards of 1990, Reform's program was bold, if not revolutionary. The best evidence of this was that there were no other established political parties in Canada (or in the United States or Britain) at this time willing to promote such a wide-ranging anti–status quo program. Moreover, as noted, in the late 1980s, Reform was even offside with public opinion, which did not yet regard deficits and fiscal policy as major concerns. Yet even by the mid-1990s, when voters were worried about provincial and federal deficits, Reform was still the only federal party proposing such a radical approach to reshaping government. Preston Manning's band of revolutionaries were thus truly the pioneering force behind neoconservative economics in Canada.

By the early years of this decade, Reform's ideas were gaining ground with the Canadian electorate, and not just in the West. In 1993, seven in ten Canadians believed that tackling the deficit was more pressing than spending money to stimulate the economy. That thinking held sway even though Canada had been in a deep recession for two years and the unemployment rate stood at over 11 percent.[12] More important, the deficit reduction agenda had now transcended political affiliation, as over three-quarters of Reform and Conservative supporters and over two-thirds of Bloc Québécois and Liberal voters wanted the deficit reduced via spending cuts.[13] By 1993 even 57 percent of NDP supporters desired deficit reduction, a statistic that may have given Bob Rae some comfort as he cut $2 billion from Ontario's public sector that year under the much-maligned "Social Contract."

The economic downturn of 1991-92 hit central Canada especially hard. Economists, opposition parties, and the media increasingly viewed the recession as policy-induced, blaming the bleak economic situation on the Mulroney government, the Bank of Canada, and fiscally profligate provincial governments, particularly the Ontario New Democrats.[14] Mulroney's critics noted that the Tories had been totally incapable of tackling the deficit and this, in conjunction with some major economic policy initiatives such as the Canada-U.S. Free Trade Agreement, the advent of the Bank's price stability policy, and the Goods and Services Tax,[15] caused a tidal wave of adjustment problems for the economy, especially in Ontario's manufacturing heartland, swelling the unemployment rolls back up to the 11 percent rate of the early 1980s.[16] This was fertile political ground for a new party like Reform, running as it was on a unique anti-government agenda based on fiscal soundness.

When viewed from this context, the neophyte party's impressive showing in the 1993 election is not surprising. Reform had been hovering at around 10 percent in most polls, but on election day the party managed to secure 18 percent of the popular vote, which was enough to increase their Parliamentary seat count from one to 52, a seat shy of making them the Official Opposition. Although all of these MPs, with one exception, were located in Western Canada, Reform, riding its right-wing economic agenda, came second in 56 ridings in Ontario and, more importantly, took 20.1 percent of the popular vote in the province. This was no mean feat given that Reform had no roots and little organization in Ontario, a region with a historically moderate electorate not given to either populist or ideological political parties.

However, after several years of profligate government under the Peterson Liberals and Rae New Democrats (the latter were responsible for a $12.4 billion deficit in 1992-93, the largest in Ontario history; Courchene and Telmer call the Rae interregnum a "fiscalamity") and two decades of big deficits in Ottawa, coupled with a recession and double-digit unemployment at the beginning of the decade, many Ontarians began to shift to the right on fiscal and economic matters. Reform may not have been responsible for this conservative tack, but it undoubtedly influenced the trend and certainly capitalized on it to win votes in the 1993 election.

Immediately after the 1993 election and throughout the first Chrétien mandate, Reform's economic conservatism was centre-stage, as Manning and his front benchers relentlessly pounded the Liberals for not moving fast enough on deficit reduction. Reform advocated a plan that would balance the federal budget by 1999, while the Liberals refused to commit themselves beyond their moderate plan to reduce the deficit to 3 percent of gross domestic product (in the final analysis the Liberals balanced the budget in 1998). By December 1994, several months after Paul Martin's first budget, opinion surveys indicated that the vast majority of Canadians were worried about the deficit; 50 percent were very concerned (a 19 percent increase from six years earlier), and a further 33 percent were somewhat concerned.[17] At this point the public did not think much of Martin's deficit-cutting skills; only 6 percent of Canadians in late 1994 indicated they had confidence in the way the Chrétien Liberals were handling the deficit.[18] Reform, of course, capitalized on this weakness. Martin, who the left-of-centre members of the Liberal caucus felt was too preoccupied with the government's balance sheet, was berated daily in the House of Commons by Manning and Herb Grubel, the Reform finance critic, for going too slow on deficit reduction.

By early 1995, surveys showed that 27 percent of Canadians thought government deficits and debt were the most important problems for Canadians. That was compared to 4 percent who felt health care, that allegedly defining feature of Canadian nationalism, should be the primary concern of government.[19] Western Canadians, not surprisingly, were fiscally more hard-line, with 47 percent indicating that deficit reduction should get top priority in Ottawa.[20] It is probably no coincidence that 1995 was also the year when Martin, no stranger to public opinion research, brought down the toughest budget in Canadian history, effectively breaking the back of the deficit through wide-ranging spending cuts, even in sacred Liberal areas like health care, education, and social assistance transfers.

Thanks to his spending cuts and a booming economy, Martin successfully fended off the left wing of the Liberal caucus and slew the deficit dragon more quickly than anyone thought possible. That robbed Reform of its main club with which to thump the Liberals. So, like any good strategist, Manning led Reform headlong onto other neoconservative economic terrain, such as debt reduction and tax cuts. The major elements of Reform's 1996 manifesto, entitled *A Fresh Start for Canadians*, reflected this shift by calling for a debt retirement program, a 50 percent reduction in capital gains taxes, a 28 percent cut in employers' UI premiums, the elimination of federal surtaxes, an increase in the basic personal and spousal exemptions, and a $2000 tax cut for the average Canadian family by the year 2000.[21] The deficit battle now over, Manning was prepared to embark upon the next and more fundamental neoconservative crusade, tax reform, the raison d'être of the Reform Party today.

THE TIDE RECEDES

By the late 1990s, it became increasingly clear that the political limits of the Reform economic agenda had been reached. The 1997 federal election was an unmitigated disaster for the party, though they achieved a key goal, beating out the Bloc Québécois in numbers of Parliamentary seats and becoming the Official Opposition. Not surprisingly, Reform held onto its dominance in Western Canada. But, in Ontario and Atlantic Canada, the party bombed, failing to win a single riding and losing the one seat they had won in Ontario in 1993. (Reform did not compete in Quebec in this election.) More importantly, Reform's share of the popular vote had not increased beyond the 20 percent or so that they had obtained four years earlier.

This turn of events was surprising to many observers because, by 1995, it seemed the neocon steamroller was unstoppable. That year Ontario voters elected the provincial Tories, led by the newest neo-conservative leader, Mike Harris, who ran on a platform essentially confined to balancing the budget, cutting taxes, and paring back social programs. By 1997, however, after two years of Harris's confrontational slash-and-burn administration, Ontarians began to come to grips with the shortcomings of his agenda. Unwilling to repeat this experiment federally, they turned their backs on Reform, and this was reflected in the party's poor showing in the province in the 1997 federal election.

The message is now clear: deficit reduction and tax cuts alone are an inadequate vision or agenda for most Canadians in the late 1990s. The sands have shifted again and this is not just a result of the fact that the war against the deficit has been basically won in most provincial capitals and in Ottawa. Witness Ontario where, even though the Harris government has failed to balance the budget and continues to run among the largest deficits in Ontario history, Ontario voters are cool to further spending cuts, which may explain why Harris talked almost as much about health care and education as tax cuts during the 1999 provincial election. An Angus Reid poll during that election indicated that 53 percent of Ontario residents would rather have Queen's Park forget about a tax cut and spend more on health and education.[22]

This indicates a new trend spawned by neoconservative economic policy. Voters are now becoming increasingly concerned about the state of Canada's health care and education systems, which everyone thought were deteriorating in part due to the deficit fight by both levels of government. In economic terms, it is becoming more and more obvious that a program confined to balancing budgets, reducing the size of government, and cutting taxes is not the panacea the neocons made it out to be and was, in fact, to blame for aggravating other problems in Canada's cherished public health care and education systems. New right economics has proven to be good at solving the fiscal problem. But it has not done anything to upgrade the quality of Canada's workforce or move the country along the way towards the knowledge-based economy of the twenty-first century, and Canadians seem to recognize this fact.

By the late 1990s, after a ten-year ascendancy, the Reform Party and its conservative economic agenda have hit the wall and are now in decline. Canadians are now groping around for something more from government than balancing the cheque book; preferably something that holds out solutions to the problems of health care, education, and joblessness and provides some road map to the future.

CONCLUSION

Neoconservatism *à la* Reform had succeeded in putting fiscal policy, the welfare state, and the size of government front and centre on the public agenda for the first time in the post-war period. Reform's rhetoric throughout the late '80s and early '90s played a major role in making some Canadians demand, and many others at least grudgingly accept, a more conservative approach to economic management, in the effort to tackle the deficit. Partly as a result of Reform's prodding, when elected in 1993, the Chrétien government abandoned progressive but expensive elements of their Red Book campaign manifesto, like public daycare, in favour of more vigorous action on the deficit front, which led to the surprising budget surplus of 1997-98, the first in thirty years. Neoconservative economics had come of age in Canada federally, thanks in no small part to Preston Manning and the Reform Party. But today this ideology is in decline on the federal scene. In the provincial capitals, however, conservative economics has played a key role in the political lives of Canada's two richest provinces: Alberta and Ontario.

TWO
CANADA'S GEMINI TWINS

A DETOUR IN ONTARIO'S POLITICAL ROAD

When Mike Harris pushed his way to the front of his campaign headquarters in North Bay, Ontario, on June 8, 1995, the new premier of Canada's largest province looked like every other politician from the beginning of time. There was the friendly wave, a kind of Huck Finn–like gesture, the slightly goofy grin, the pointing at people in the audience as if he and his wife had just discovered a large number of long-lost friends in the room . . . which they probably had.

For many analysts, however, Harris's upset victory represented a watershed, a new era in Ontario. The central Canadian province had been known for its middle-of-the-road governments. This is where the Tory premier Bill Davis governed for so many years, running an administration better known for its fuzzy, feel-good quality than its hard ideological edges.

Now, Ontarians were about to be introduced to Harris and the Common Sense Revolution, a policy blueprint as right-wing as they have ever seen in that province. Fashioned by such hard-nosed conservatives as the executive search consultant Tom Long and the lobbyist Leslie Noble, the CSR laid out a plan to cut income taxes by a whopping 30 percent, balance the budget almost within one term, slash welfare payments by about 20 percent, and eliminate heaps of government regulation, all in the name of freeing up the private sector.

The election of the Conservatives caught many people off-guard. Political observers had expected Lyn McLeod and her bland band of Liberals to ease their way into the seat of power. Instead, Ontario voters got Harris's crowd and their take-no-prisoners approach to government. The province braced itself for a battle between entrenched groups who benefited from public largesse and a government, much like Richard Nixon's administration, that claimed to be standing up for the silent majority — that overtaxed, under-appreciated group that made Ontario the most prosperous region in Canada.

Harris and his party fell into their hard-right position by accident, not as part of a well-thought-out political campaign — not as the U.S. Republican heavyweight Newt Gingrich did with his Contract with America in 1994. Indeed, the Tories assembled the pieces of a coherent campaign and then spent the five years in opposition trying out different themes until they found one that worked.

In the 1995 vote, Harris built upon the "tax fighter" mantle that he had gained during the 1990 provincial election. Back then, he was battling for his political life against David Peterson's supposedly invincible Liberals and Bob Rae's achingly earnest New Democrats. Harris struck a distinctly conservative pose, promising to chop the province's high taxes, as a survival tactic in a vote in which the Tories' main goal was to retain official party status. In the end, it worked; the Tories grabbed

20 seats, while Rae's NDP won a surprise majority government and the Liberals were banished back to the opposition benches.

BOB RAE'S SORRY LEGACY

Very quickly, however, Rae's government became a good example of how times had changed for public officials.

When his group came unexpectedly to power in 1990, Ontario was already showing signs of slipping into a recession. By the time Floyd Laughren, the treasurer, presented his first budget a year later, the government's finances had deteriorated at a rate similar to the economy.

As a result, Laughren announced a stunning $10.9 billion deficit in his 1991 budget, three times its previous record. Back then, Rae said it was more important to fight the province's rising jobless rate through massive public stimulus than it was to please Bay Street and Wall Street bondholders. That was not a sound theory in these "Keynes is dead" times, when some suspender-snapping yuppie on a brokerage trading floor moving money around the globe electronically can have almost as much influence upon a province's financial health as a premier. After Laughren's budget, Ontario was quickly downgraded by U.S. credit agencies and the province became a pariah among economic analysts.

Of course, almost every government, including that of Ronald Reagan, has gone through a period where its policies have not been particularly popular with global financiers.

In Rae's case, however, the wickedly high deficit reinforced the view among money professionals and many voters that an NDP government had no idea how to run an economy effectively. As a result, no matter what he and his comrades did in the next four years to get Ontario's finances in better shape, they never lost the reputation of being a well-intentioned but incompetent bunch of economic managers, a sort of governmental version of Andy Griffith's Barney Fife. Once proven to be financial nincompoops, any other policy the NDP implemented looked silly at best and criminal at worst. An employment equity law that caught businesses in a morass of red tape, a labour law that courted employee unrest, and a workers' compensation program that paid people more money to stay home than to return to the job all became examples of government naïveté. Everything Rae did was seen in the light of the first huge fiscal deficit.

Rae's descent into public policy hell became a lesson for every other politician across Canada. Get your deficit under control, or at least look like you are doing so, or risk being tarred as an out-of-touch government ready to spend money with no idea when or how to stop.

Partly because of Rae's example and partly because North America's financiers offered no alternative, most Canadian governments began cutting their deficits substantially. Saskatchewan's Roy Romanow was the first premier to get his province's bottom line back up to zero. Every other province has followed suit, except for B.C. and, surprisingly, Ontario.

Back in the early '90s, however, Harris's course of action became clear. Rev up the tax fighter message, pound cost-cutting reforms to social programs, and get the conservative word out to his key voting group, older white males, especially in the suburban belt around Toronto.

What had begun as the path of survival now looked like a possible victory strategy. As he embarked upon his right turn, Harris had prominent models from which to draw practical lessons.

In the United States, there was Ronald Reagan's joyous administration when Republicans could do no wrong and the best leaders liberals could muster were Walter Mondale and Michael Dukakis. In Britain, it was Thatcher and her brand of tough individualism, a much-preferable option to Labour's incredibly feeble Michael Foot.

IN THE BEGINNING, THERE WAS RALPH

And, in Canada, there was Ralph Klein, the Liberal-turned-Tory, radio-broadcaster-turned-politician. Klein became the shining star of Canada's neoconservative movement after he was first elected Alberta's premier in 1993.

At a time when Brian Mulroney's federal Tories and the provincial governments across the country appeared to be skilled only at creating debt, not buoyant economies, Klein was a Rock of Gibraltar. This unusual politician was able to tame a runaway budget, kick large batches of welfare shirkers out of the province, and get Alberta's economy growing faster. Even liberals gave him a measure of grudging respect.

Here is a real, on-the-ground example of Canada's conservative movement in action. While Preston Manning brought these ideas to the public stage in the late 1980s, Klein was the first premier or prime minister to implement notions of free market economics and fiscal prudence to get an economy moving again. Harris started beating the right-wing drum earlier than the Alberta premier, but only in opposition. Klein became the litmus test against which other administrations in Canada came to be measured.

Rarely was there a man who appeared to fit the politician's mould less. Born in Calgary in 1942, Klein was the son of a one-time professional wrestler, Phil "The Killer" Klein, but was raised by his grandparents after his father and mother were divorced. To say his formative years were nondescript would be an understatement.

Klein dropped out of school in Grade 10 at the age of seventeen to join the Royal Canadian Air Force. He eventually graduated from the Alberta Business School, where he stayed on to teach and wound up as principal. In 1963, Klein took a job as public relations director for the Alberta Red Cross and then, three years later, for the United Way. His first experience in politics was in 1968, under the Liberal banner, handling the publicity in a failed bid by Calgary alderman and lawyer Peter Petrusak for a federal seat.

The next year, Klein took a job at Calgary's CFCN as a radio reporter, staying on to become municipal issues specialist on local television. As an aside, it is surprising how many conservative politicians worked for the same non-business institutions as did liberals. Klein was a reporter, usually a breeding ground for Liberal and NDP types. Harris started off as a teacher, although he did run a small business. Manning was a business consultant, a dispenser of advice rather than a risk taker. Reagan was an actor. Gingrich, Phil Gramm, a prominent conservative Texas senator, and Dick Armey, a Texas Republican congressman, were all university professors, institutions usually believed to be hotbeds of liberal thought.

IF YOU DON'T LIKE YOUR DAYTIME JOB . . .

Klein ran for mayor of Calgary in 1980 on a whim, using his last remaining $300 to take a run at the incumbent, Ross Alger, whom he had criticized consistently while working as a reporter.

Klein's campaign was viewed as so wingy that his own station manager thought he was kidding. After all, you are talking about a man who chose as his key adviser a restaurant waiter, Rod Love.

But Klein won the city's top job with 47 percent of the vote, defeating Alger. He boosted his electoral majority in 1986, about the same time he became famous for referring to people who migrated to Calgary from out of Alberta as "creeps" and "bums."

On the plus side of the ledger, Klein brought the 1988 Olympics to his city, enhancing Calgary's image. He was a man with the common touch. No fancy lunches and expensive suits; instead, Klein held court in the St. Louis Hotel near City Hall, where he would hoist a few and talk about whatever was on his mind.

Eventually, however, the boredom of running Calgary and the possibility of a provincial cabinet post enticed Klein to throw his hat into that arena in 1989. At the time, the oil patch province had the increasingly aloof Don Getty as premier. In fact, Tories had dominated the political scene here ever since Peter Lougheed won in 1971, defeating Harry Strom's Social Credit Party, 55 seats to 25 seats.

By the early '90s, Getty's Conservative machine was in need of a tune-up. The government kept running larger and larger deficits in the face of slowing tax revenues and falling oil prices. As well, Getty's administration kept promoting questionable economic forecasts in a bid to show that Alberta was in better financial shape than was actually the case.

Meanwhile, Klein was made environment minister upon entering provincial politics in 1989. He soldiered on in this unfamiliar portfolio, carving out a respectable enough record to allow him to run for Getty's job three years later.

Again media types underestimated Klein's political acumen. The winner of that convention was expected to be another Tory minister, Nancy Betkowski. She was supposed to update the image of the too-male-dominated Progressive Conservative Party and attract more young urban voters.

By the early 1990s, Alberta looked to be on the verge of a sea change. The Liberals, under the former Edmonton mayor Laurence Decore, were gaining popularity and many Conservatives believed Betkowski was the only person who could keep the party in power.

In this fray, Klein was an outsider, more appealing in the rural areas than in the cities, but not a serious contender to beat Decore. Klein pushed a common man image, organized heavily, and won the Conservative leadership.

He soon faced an election and a crabby electorate. Under Getty, Alberta's books had become seriously out of whack. The province's debt had grown to $15 billion by 1992-93 with a deficit approaching $3.5 billion, a huge shortfall given Alberta's economic size. To shrink the deficit, both Klein and Decore pledged big cuts and, as an example of how conservative voters were becoming, the Liberal leader won the war of words by describing his chopping as "brutal," trumping Klein's modestly described "massive" reductions.

Thanks to Ralph's easy manner and the Tories' long time in power and stellar organization, his party won the PC's seventh consecutive majority government, grabbing 51 out of 83 seats, or 62 percent of the seats in the legislature, with only 45 percent of the popular vote.

KING KLEIN

Once ensconced as premier, Klein quickly went about making good on his promise of fiscal austerity. Everything went under his government's financial knife: MPPs' pensions gone, welfare benefits slashed, hospitals closed, children's education programs scrapped. During the next couple of years, Klein went on an economic holy war.

By April 1994, more than 143,000 people had been heaved off the welfare rolls. In fact, B.C.'s government started complaining that Klein's cuts were driving people into Lotus Land in search of a better deal.

In the same year, the government promised to cut $1.5 billion from education, health, and social services. Liquor stores were privatized. And, in a move echoed by Harris four years later, Klein's government seized control of education financing and took away from school boards their power to raise money through the property tax.

If the most important goal of the exercise was to eliminate the province's deficit, the plan worked, helped by firming world oil prices. While Alberta ran nine consecutive deficits between fiscal 1985-86 and 1993-94, Klein balanced the books by the next year and, in 1997-98, the province posted its third surplus in a row, more than $2 billion.

Interestingly, the tone of Klein's government changed while the province stayed in the black. As Alberta entered the latter part of the decade, the government was no longer bragging about its campaign of clear-cutting social programs. Instead, Klein's Tories cancelled the final year of health care cuts and restored funding to kindergarten.

Besides deciding to improve the funding of some social services, Alberta also backed off of its promise to wipe out its accumulated debt. Initially, Klein indicated he wanted to eliminate all provincial debt within twenty-five years. Soon that line in the sand turned into a vague notion of reducing the red ink by one-quarter within the same time period, not bad compared to the rest of Canada's jurisdictions, but still less ambitious than Albertans had originally been promised.

Throughout his time in power, Klein had steadfastly refused to implement a major tax cut. He had even gone so far as to call on Harris to drop that part of the Ontario premier's policy program.

Then, in his 1999 budget, Klein finally moved on taxes. He promised to bring in an 11 percent single-rate tax system by 2002. The government's move would be an approximately 10 percent tax reduction. But the province has pledged to make these changes only if Alberta's economy grows at a rate greater than 3 percent in real terms in the interim, an obvious escape hatch.

In fact, some analysts have speculated that the strange introduction date of this single-tax regime was a way to enhance the profile of Stockwell Day, the Alberta treasurer, who is running against Manning for the leadership of the United Alternative party.

Alberta continues to enjoy the lowest tax rates in the country and a booming economy. Klein has no reason to risk his province's fiscal future by cutting his revenue base for an unlikely economic gain. Besides, Klein was never elected on a pledge to cut taxes. And, in politics, there is little sense in implementing such fundamental changes unless compelled to do so by past utterances.

HARRIS TRIES ON KLEIN'S SUIT WITH SOME ALTERATIONS

It is a bit early to say whether Mike Harris is returning to the political centre in the same manner as Klein. During the 1999 election campaign, he stuck to the familiar themes of tax cuts and taking shots at welfare recipients. At the same time, Harris has distanced himself from more radical policies, such as school vouchers, private health care, and privately owned transit.

When he grabbed power in 1995, Harris took a page from Klein's political book and implemented election promises at breath-taking speed. The Tories unceremoniously yanked union rights installed under Bob Rae. They slashed welfare rates by 21 percent and redefined who can get these benefits, pushing a large portion of formerly eligible people off social assistance lists. A convoluted NDP policy supposed to ensure that minorities and women did not face job discrimination was chucked out the window.

To be sure, all this was not done without a share of protests and civil unrest. In 1996, the Harris government endured a nasty civil service strike as it started to implement a program to reduce the public payrolls. The next year saw the Conservatives annoy many Torontonians by jamming the area's municipalities into one "megacity." Last year, the government saw teachers walk off the job over education reforms and, in 1999, school technical staff went on strike for more money.

As the Tories put in place these hard-nosed policies, the aim was not to balance the budget. Of course, Harris genuflected towards the gods of fiscal rectitude, arguing that his administration would eliminate the deficit.

The big-ticket item for his government, however, is its 30 percent provincial income tax cut. Put in place as a way of differentiating themselves from the provincial Liberals, the Tories sold the estimated $4 billion tax cut on the grounds that consumers would spend more and stimulate the economy. The Conservatives would slice one-third off the provincial rate to bring Ontario's income tax level below Alberta's.

The Tories, however, also implemented a health related surtax to collect some of that money back from wealthier taxpayers. As well, Queen's Park and Ontario municipalities cranked up user fees for just about everything. But, on the bottom line, everyone in Harris's Ontario would receive a tax break.

Ironically, such thinking could only be described as Keynesian. Harris did not pretend his tax cut was a supply-side-like measure that would unleash massive amounts of pent-up entrepreneurial energy in response to the lower rates. The Tories' reduction would simply put more cash in people's pockets and help retail sales. Cutting taxes to boost consumption is right out of basic Keynes.

To finance this reduction, Harris promised to balance the budget by the fiscal year 2000-2001, after the next election and far more slowly than other provincial regimes.

The first budget of the Conservative treasurer Ernie Eves was in 1994-95 and produced a deficit of $8.8 billion. Now that was a good 13 percent improvement over the previous year. Things got even better in the next few years as the Tories averaged a 20 percent reduction in the deficit in the next 36 months.

With all the pain that Ontarians had endured, however, the province still has a $2 billion shortfall. Although the Tories probably will balance their books this year, they could have done so earlier if they had forgone the tax cut.

AFTER FOUR YEARS OF PAIN, WHAT IS THE GAIN?

Ontario's economy has hummed along under Harris. The province grew at an average clip of 3.25 percent during the past four years and created more than 600,000 jobs in five. And, unlike Alberta's, Ontario's economy is not subject to swings in oil prices. Indeed, while Alberta faces a bit of slow going because of record rock-bottom crude prices, Ontario chugs along benefiting from rock-bottom commodity prices and a falling Canadian dollar.

So, how much credit should the Tories get for all this good economic news and how much is blind luck? Certainly, Harris benefited from the fact that he was not Bob Rae. The province's private sector felt so battered by five years of Rae's unfriendly policies that any non-NDP person, animal, or inanimate object who occupied the premier's chair was going to be a winner as far as the business community was concerned.

The Conservatives get some accolades for getting the red ink down. Right now, the deficit has dropped substantially and, with it, the rate at which the province is accumulating debt.

Unfortunately, this indicator is not Harris's best. In the past nine years, only British Columbia, led by the spectacularly incompetent Glen Clark, and Ontario are the only provinces not to have been in the black at least once.

Of course, few supporters or critics doubt the Ontario Tories' commitment to reach this fiscal promised land. But its so-so fiscal record is unlikely to be the best drawing card in attracting the attention of North America's notoriously impersonal financial markets. Interestingly, bond-rating agencies, those groups that check the creditworthiness of companies and governments on both sides of the border, did not improve Ontario's credit rating in Harris's first term.

That makes Ontario's tax cut more important than ever. In Klein's case, the assurance that his party would continue Alberta's small-c conservative economic policies plus his commitment to eliminating the deficit were enough to win him awards as the most pro-business government in Canada.

In central Canada, Harris has no such legacy upon which to rely. Instead, he needed to follow through on his promises no matter what. While politically the tax cut was crucial, to explain Ontario's improvement by this measure is questionable economics.

For the cut to work properly, consumers would have to spend more and companies would have to set up shop here to take advantage of the new demand. But the Conservatives diluted their own tax cut by implementing a health care levy that accumulated at the higher income levels. That reduced some of the positive impact of the tax reduction.

The Tories also ran into a problem of Ottawa's doing. In 1998, the Liberals boosted individual deductions for the Canada Pension Plan. The pay-as-you-go program was faced with huge outlays in the near future as Canada's baby boomers get set to retire. As a result, Paul Martin dinged Canadians for extra contributions to cover the higher costs.

To the economy, a dollar is a dollar. Which level of government taxes or spends does not matter. It makes no difference whether Harris or Chrétien raised taxes. People will react in economic terms in roughly the same way.

In this case, the CPP contribution soaked up some of Ontario's tax reduction, which partly explains why Harris opposed the pension increase and demanded an offsetting employment insurance cut from Ottawa. What was supposed to be $4.5 billion injected into the provincial economy shrank.

Worse still, Canada has suffered from high real interest rates (borrowing costs after subtracting the effects of inflation) throughout the 1990s. That means that the ability of companies to pay off their outstanding debts has decreased relative to their product selling prices and that the ability of individuals to buy new goods and services has fallen relative to their pay levels.

For both these reasons, the purchasing power of Ontarians, through no fault of Mike Harris, has dropped. That left the positive effects of the province's large income tax cut as a political, not an economic, bragging point.

Still, Harris's Tories have a good story to sell voters: unemployment down, growth up, the deficit decreasing, and prospects up. They have no real economic theory to back their plan up, however. There was no supply-side entrepreneurial burst from the tax cuts. Ontarians did spend more on consumer and other goods as Harris's administration predicted. But so did other Canadians, even those ones who did not receive a tax cut.[1]

As an economic proposition, all that can be said with confidence is that the Tories kept Ontario from sliding backwards.

The government also chopped union power by reworking the province's labour code. During the first term of the government, however, the number of days lost due to work stoppages jumped.

The removal of substantial amounts of useless government regulation may have helped the provincial economy. Much of the advice on what to remove, however, came from the red tape commission, a group that has reported only recently, making any economic boost from fewer rules marginal at this point.

In all these cases, the economic effects of the Harris platform appear to be less than advertised.

THE SMILE FACTOR

In fact, Harris's government has benefited from two major external trends. The U.S. economy continues to race ahead like a powerful thoroughbred charging to the finish line of a race in which it is already leading. U.S. growth is going along at a 4 percent clip and that country's unemployment rate has crashed below the 5 percent level, something thought unimaginable only a few years ago.

With more than 80 percent of its trade heading south, Canada was able to hitch itself to the American economy, boosting its own prospects. Not surprisingly, Ontario's economic fortunes also climbed by its proximity to the American market, especially in the free trade and low dollar environment of the past decade.

As well, Harris was not Rae, whose mere appearance caused men in suits to start booing. Harris is seen as the saviour of capitalism in this province. Everywhere he went, employers applauded, investors whistled, and bankers cheered. These good feelings were translated into a renewed confidence concerning Ontario's economic prospects.

If political language embodies the kind of government a politician would lead, Harris has shown again and again that he is interested in promoting a strong, private-sector-oriented jurisdiction. From the business community's perspective, that is Harris's biggest strength. He has followed through on most of his economic promises and continues to mouth the proper words to inspire confidence.

Harris has, however, spent a large chunk of his first term annoying interest groups, such as the public sector unions, teachers, some parents, health care professionals, and most of the City of Toronto. Taken individually, voters might applaud the smacking around of the education unions or smug taxpayers in downtown Toronto. But together these confrontations stamp the government as one that courts open fights with opponents, that is trying to get its agenda through no matter the cost, and that wants to reduce the size of government programs — any government programs — as quickly as possible.

Harris faces two problems for the future. He is running out of obvious enemies. Some groups have already been tamed by past pummelling; others believe they have been picked on enough by the government and want the fighting stopped. In the 1999 election, the best Harris could do was a minor, albeit offensive, promise to force welfare recipients to undergo drug rehabilitation, based upon the results of random drug testing.

THE SECOND TIME AROUND IS NEVER EASY

Perhaps more serious, however, are the issues upon which voters have expressed the strongest disagreements with the government: education and health care. Here Harris talks tough but is seen as less competent.

So far, he has compared nursing to making hula hoops. He has provoked one teachers' strike in which his government looked marginally at fault, and another among the support staff. Now voters have a hard time seeing the Tories as anything but hard-nosed, or maybe mean-spirited, in these areas.

According to public opinion polls in early 1999, Ontarians view fixing the education and medical systems in the province as the most important issues, by a wide margin. And the same pollsters said that many voters were looking for someone with Harris's iron will, but encasing a beating, not a stone, heart.[2]

Reading these tea leaves, Harris bowed a bit to the inevitable and began to move ever so slowly towards the political centre. Last winter, his government started running ads talking about its accomplishments in health care and explaining why it was not the bad guy during the bitter teachers' strike. Elizabeth Witmer, the health minister, began throwing money around like confetti, finding additional bucks for cancer care units, emergency rooms, and new nurses.

Indeed, Harris's was one of the strongest provincial voices recently pushing Ottawa to increase its health care transfers to the provinces.

There were still some policy bones for his right-wing supporters in the 1999 campaign, such as calls to reform the federal Young Offenders Act and a move to force teenage welfare mothers to finish school. In addition, he talked about the need to enforce discipline in the class-room through the introduction of school uniforms and other tough measures.

The re-election road for Ontario's Tories was clear. Fiddle on the edges of the tax system, this time with two 20 percent cuts from differ-ent taxes. That was to show core voters that their administration still understands how to keep an economy going. But start looking warm and fuzzy on the social spending side. No more "Mr. Tough Guy." It's time to put on that old Perry Como cardigan, break out the pipe, and start talking like a well-meaning uncle.

The Tories needed to go this route essentially because another big tax cut likely risked bringing up visions of more strikes, public service reductions, and increased anxieties concerning whether the local hos-pital and school would stay open.

Part of Harris's calculation was political, trying to give voters a fresh agenda without retracing too many old steps. Some of this math was economic. After years of cuts, the party had nothing to offer to keep the Ontario economic miracle going. Tax cuts are no longer credible as a financial supercharger, if they ever were. Indeed, in 1999, Harris had not even the semblance of economic theory to support his proposed 20 percent tax cut. This time he only had a stale prop in the form of a glass jar full of loonies to show the benefit to taxpayers of his programs. Also, any further degradation of the province's ability to maintain its revenues threatens Ontario's attack on the deficit if the economy hits a downturn.

The removal of more regulation only begs the question why these were not eliminated during Harris's first go-round. And the same logic would apply to further labour law reform.

KLEIN AND HARRIS HIT THE SAME BUMP IN THE ROAD

These days, both these conservative premiers, Klein and Harris, have hit the same barrier. Having reduced their deficits and, in Ontario's case, taxes, they do not have a strong agenda for the next few years. Many remaining conservative policies are increasingly tough sells to the electorates in the two provinces. As a result, both premiers seem more interested in rebuilding their social safety nets with budgetary surpluses than in attacking welfare, health, and education any more. Ontario and Alberta already enjoy the lowest provincial tax rates in the land, making any further cuts here more likely to cause harm than good. And neither Klein nor Harris really has much to say about developing human capital.

Instead, both men, like Chrétien in Ottawa, are hunkering down, finding the most politically saleable policies instead of ones that might assist their provinces' longer-term prospects. They believe that freeing up the market and lowering public levies are all there is to economic policy.

That may have been true for thirty years. In the new information age of the 1990s, they are mistaken.

*T*HREE

MUDDLING THROUGH WITH JEAN CHRÉTIEN'S LIBERALS

Crossroads. Fork in the Road. Point of Inflection. Shifting Tide. All these clichés could be applied to Jean Chrétien's Liberals in 1999. But they all boil down to one thing. "Which way will Chrétien turn?" as a newspaper headline screamed.[1] And Canadians really would like to know. For a party priding itself on having a big tent, Chrétien's cloth canvas seems to encompass everyone's point of view . . . and, at the same time, no one's.

The Liberal Party of Canada has always been a non-ideological institution. That does not mean Liberals lack core values. They go to great lengths to emphasize compassion, tolerance, and fairness, values that have been reflected in many Liberal policies over the years. However, the federal Liberal Party is not as wedded to or identified with particular ideologies or currents of thought as their rivals, the Progressive Conservative, New Democratic, and Reform parties. Liberals might support an affirmative action policy one day and oppose that policy the next, as long as, in both cases, the party can persuade itself that its core value of fairness is upheld. Other parties believe that a particular policy almost always reflects a basic belief. The Liberal party, by contrast, tends to be more evidence-driven. If the facts point in one direction, so will the party.

Critics regard this type of non-philosophy as unprincipled, weak-kneed, or populist. Supporters, however, point out that the Grits, more than the other parties, are able to adapt to modern times and changing circumstances. The most commonly cited illustration of the Liberals' lack of ideology is their vacillating position on free trade over the past century, although the Tories have also changed their minds on this subject a few times. Liberals are not populist, but they are flexible and have tried throughout their history, with a great deal of success, to promote agendas that fit with the times.

This flexibility has been, arguably, the party's greatest electoral strength and competitive advantage. After all, most Canadians see themselves as pragmatic, not apt to be taken in by the false promises of ideology. So why wouldn't the party that has dominated federal politics in Canada during the twentieth century reflect the same thinking? That is the key reason why Liberals can, and do, regard themselves, with equal parts arrogance and truth, as Canada's natural governing party.

After the Second World War, however, the Liberal Party came to be identified with big, interventionist government, principally because the administrations of Mackenzie King, Louis St. Laurent, Lester Pearson, and Pierre Trudeau, which governed for most of this period, built Canada's welfare state and followed increasingly interventionist economic and industrial policies, vastly pumping up the size and scope of the federal government. Nevertheless, it was not until the late 1970s that Liberals became tagged as fiscally profligate, due to a decade of rising annual deficits under Trudeau. (The real heavy lifting that built the welfare state was done by Trudeau's predecessors, but they tended to deliver balanced budgets or, on occasion, very small deficits.)

The Liberals' love for big government, however, was not a consequence of any firm attachment to bloated bureaucracies or a statist ideology. Rather, it reflected the belief of most politicians that the big-spending approach to economic management had merit and, more importantly, the fact that this approach was in vogue throughout the industrialized world in the 1950s, '60s, and '70s. During these years you could not get within spitting distance of electoral victory without bowing to the gods of government spending, or pump-priming. And the federal Liberals, probably more than most Canadian political parties, don't like to buck international trends that have strong domestic appeal.

When Jean Chrétien, the "little guy from Shawinigan," who cut his political teeth under Lester Pearson and held eight ministerial portfolios during the Trudeau years, became prime minister in 1993, most people assumed that his government would follow in the big-spending, economic-interventionist footsteps of his mentors. During the 1993 election Chrétien constantly waved in front of the television cameras the Liberals' campaign manifesto called *Creating Opportunity* (commonly known as the "Red Book") as the plan his government would follow if elected. A quick glance at the Red Book seemed to confirm that a Chrétien government would be anything but fixated on the deficit. The document talked about solving unemployment through new spending programs, in such areas as daycare, youth employment, infrastructure development, education, training, apprenticeships, research and development, and small-business financing. Has anyone been left out here? The industrial strategies of the famous (or infamous, depending on your orientation) Japanese Ministry of International Trade and Industry (MITI) were touted, signalling that the Liberals were planning to head back down the road of greater government involvement in the economy.[2] A mild deficit-fighting program was mentioned, but almost as an afterthought. Nor was it to push out other, people-oriented commitments that were more in keeping with the Pearson-Trudeau legacies of active government.

To many people, a Chrétien government of this ilk was a certainty. The Red Book was not a project that had been imposed by the left wing of the party that would be jettisoned once the Liberals took power. Instead, the principal architect of this manifesto was Paul Martin Jr., corporate executive, finance minister in waiting, and leader of the party's business wing. If he was backing this bit of political eye candy, then consider its implementation a done deal once Chrétien reached 24 Sussex Drive.

This view of the new Liberal government was further confirmed when Chrétien, after the election, appointed some left-leaning former Trudeau ministers, such as Herb Gray, Lloyd Axworthy, and David Collenette, to senior Cabinet positions. While these men did not hold the key economic portfolios of Finance, Industry, and Trade (which were occupied by Martin, John Manley, and Roy McLaren, all of whom were more pro-business Liberals), they nonetheless carried considerable weight around the Cabinet table and would keep the government from getting hijacked by a conservative economic agenda. Or so the conventional wisdom went. In addition, the PM surrounded himself with senior advisers like Eddie Goldenberg and Chaviva Hosek, both of whom were regarded as "progressive" Liberals. So all the evidence pointed to Chrétien's government taking policy back to that of its predecessors, although Martin would try to bring the deficit down to 3 percent of GDP within a few years (a number without a firm economic foundation, copied from the European Union's Maastricht Treaty).

The prospect of the new Liberal regime bringing a return to the high-spending interventionist days of past administrations was a slam dunk according to the chattering classes in the newspapers and on television and radio talk shows. Of course, these towering intellects are the same crowd who thought Quebec would never come close to quitting Canada in 1995, that Lyn McLeod would win that year's election in Ontario, and that the Spice Girls would never last. Wrong, wrong, and wrong. And they were wrong again in misjudging where the Chrétien government was headed in 1993-94.

By the fall of 1994, signs began to emerge that a change in course was in the works, and by early '95 the handwriting was on the wall. If Chrétien really had a "traditional" Liberal agenda in mind, it was going on the back burner indefinitely, in favour of a single-minded effort to eliminate the deficit. The man at the helm of the budget-cutting ship was the former Canada Steamship Lines president, Paul Martin.

PAUL MARTIN: NECESSARY NEOCONSERVATISM BUT NOT NECESSARILY BY A NEOCON

Martin was, and some people think remains in his heart, a true believer in activist government and perhaps even grand industrial strategies as the way to solve the nation's unemployment problem (Canada's unemployment rate stood at over 11 percent when the Liberals took office in 1993). Reportedly, the son of the great Liberal warhorse Paul Martin Sr. wanted the Industry portfolio, not Finance, as the route to implement his ideas and become Canada's C.D. Howe for the 1990s. Chrétien, however, said no and shoved the country's reluctant fiscal saviour into Finance. But that move did not immediately change Martin's outlook. When he took the Cabinet oath in the fall of 1993, he showed his real colours by saying, "The root cause of the deficit and the root cause of unemployment are one and the same, and that is the ailing economy."[3] Such remarks, unscripted at this point by Department of Finance bureaucrats who typically do not subscribe to such thinking, further reinforced the Red Book theme that industrial and employment policies would be the Liberal government's economic priority, permitting Canada to grow its way to fiscal health. Conspicuously absent from the new finance minister's comments was any talk of deficit reduction as a top priority. And certainly nothing was said about sharp spending cuts. This was consistent with the Liberals' campaign rhetoric, where Chrétien barely mentioned the deficit, preferring to leave Manning and Kim Campbell to pound away on this uninspiring theme, which had questionable political appeal at that point.

However, after a few months cloistered away in the fiscally conservative confines of the Department of Finance, Martin's thinking began to change. In relatively short order he developed a conviction that the overriding priority had to be deficit reduction. During these early days at Finance, Martin appeared to dump the notion that the usual grab bag of employment or industrial policies could grow the country out of its $42 billion budgetary hole. Martin's bureaucrats, especially David Dodge, his deputy and a true believer in deficit reduction, helped him reach these new conclusions. But he was also assisted in the new thinking by the former banker and intellectual heavyweight Peter Nicholson. Nicholson, at Martin's request, took up the position in Finance of Clifford Clark Visiting Economist in early 1994 to help shape what became the deficit-breaking budget of 1995. In the final analysis, Nicholson, a friend of Martin's and well-respected around Ottawa and on Bay Street for his sharp mind and agreeable demeanour, would prove to be probably the most influential visiting economist the Department of Finance had ever had.

Pragmatism had thus become the watchword early in the Chrétien mandate. Any commitment to an ideology reflecting the agendas of previous Liberal governments was abandoned in favour of a practical approach in the context of the fiscal crisis of the time. Simply put, the government wanted more forceful, focused action to eliminate the deficit. However, despite the usual carping by unions and social interest groups that the Liberals were becoming closet neocons, there was nothing ideological about this new agenda. The shift in direction was simply regarded as a necessity given the fiscal mess Canada faced in the mid-1990s. With ample help from Preston Manning and his Reform Party, who sensitized public opinion to the country's growing fiscal problem, Martin proceeded down the deficit-fighting track with a reasonable degree of voter support, something he could use in disarming his critics inside and outside government.

Relying heavily on Nicholson's eloquent pen, Martin crafted a softer, more pragmatic rationale for deficit reduction than the chest-thumping one of the Reform Party. This he could sell to his Cabinet colleagues and the Liberal caucus, who generally were not deficit crusaders and wanted the government to start meeting the Red Book spending promises. If reducing the deficit was the goal, it became politically critical to develop a compelling "Liberal" storyline for public consumption. This required carefully worded statements to convey this message, like: "The debt and deficit are often portrayed as issues primarily of concern to financial markets and ideologues. The truth is that those who suffer most immediately from Canada's fiscal deterioration are the unemployed, the poorer regions of the country, and the average young to middle-aged family with a mortgage and other debt incurred to raise and educate their children."[4] Armed with such progressive arguments for belt-tightening, the Chrétien team embarked upon what could be described as an ambivalent or reluctant conservative economic strategy, causing one senior Liberal insider to remark: "I would not dignify this government with an ideology."

WHITE AND PURPLE MAKE RED

Martin's first budget had an innocuous white cover and was brought down inauspiciously in February 1994, some four months after the Liberals took office. It was a non-event, reflecting a party still trying to find its governmental legs after nearly a decade in opposition. What the budget was notable for, however, was its recognition that Ottawa needed to set up processes leading up to the next budget that would provide a substantive way out of the impending fiscal crisis. Even after the Mulroney government posted the $42 billion deficit of 1993-94, and amidst warnings from alarmists that the IMF was about to knock at Canada's door, the Liberals, at least rhetorically, still refused to place deficit reduction at the top of their priority list. Instead, the agenda in 1994 was articulated as follows: "This budget represents the first phase of a two-stage process which will culminate in the 1995 Budget. Together, the measures in these two budgets will lead to a fundamental reform of programs in most policy areas to enhance their impact on growth and job creation, to raise their efficiency, and to secure the government's interim target of a 3 percent deficit-to-GDP ratio by 1996-97."[5]

Deficit reduction thus came second to the other Red Book commitments, many of which were funded in this budget, despite the country's $42 billion flood of red ink. The budget also showed some signs that the government was cutting expenses back by taking the easy steps of withdrawing from some megaprojects, reducing defence spending, and freezing departmental allocations. But the 1994 document contained no substantial spending cuts.

Just as the new government was grappling with the deficit, however, the Liberals took another page out of the conservative economics textbook by confirming their support for the Bank of Canada's policy of price stability. In opposition, the Liberals, including Paul Martin as the finance critic, had been vocal opponents of the tight money, zero-inflation program inaugurated a few years earlier by the Bank's governor, the acerbic and generally unpopular Englishman John Crow. During the late 1980s and early 1990s the Liberals echoed the voices of many of the Bank's critics, who argued that Crow's monetary policy was narrow-minded in its drive to stamp out inflation, that it neglected the adverse social and economic effects associated with high interest rates, principally growing unemployment.[6] However, after the symbolic dumping of Crow in favour of his second-in-command, the mild-mannered, Saskatchewan-born Gordon Thiessen, the Liberals embraced price stability as the primary objective of monetary policy and accepted the prevailing orthodoxy that very low inflation (within 1-3 percent) was the best economic medicine the Bank could prescribe for the ailing Canadian economy.

Meanwhile, the government also launched a major social policy review, under the leadership of Lloyd Axworthy, that pinkest of Liberals, in conjunction with the infamous Program Review exercise. The latter was ambitiously portrayed as a vigorous intellectual effort to rethink the whole federal government, but came to be little more than a hastily organized and poorly executed cost-cutting exercise.[7] By contrast, Axworthy's social policy review was not billed as an effort to reduce the costs of income security programs but rather as a project to make the system, in the preferred parlance of the policy wonks, more "active" and less "passive" (translation: Get the unemployed to take low-paying jobs, and get people off income support and into training and skills upgrading programs).[8] Certainly, with Axworthy at the helm, few feared that deep cuts to those cherished Liberal-designed income support programs, such as Unemployment Insurance and Old Age Security, were in the works.

Unfortunately, after several months of public debate around the so-called Green Paper,[9] Axworthy's review fell apart, due largely to internal dissension within the government on what to reform or cut, and when and how to do it. With another election or referendum in Quebec always looming, many political insiders wanted to blunt any bold ideas Axworthy might have on the social policy front rather than face potential national unity fallout. At the end of the day all he managed to achieve of substance, after sustaining numerous battle scars from Quebec and Atlantic Canadian ministers, especially Brian Tobin and David Dingwall, was the okay to tinker with the hopelessly inequitable and regionally skewed unemployment insurance system. In fact, Axworthy's most publicly visible achievement was simply to rename this program Employment Insurance.

Conversely, the low-key Program Review was all about cutting spending and in fact yielded about $9.5 billion in savings to the federal government by eliminating some programs and sharply reducing others. Each week throughout the fall of 1994, nine of Chrétien's key ministers, in addition to their regular responsibilities, were buried in paper and confined for several hours in the Cabinet committee responsible for this bureaucratic water torture, officially known as the Co-ordinating Group of Ministers on Program Review. Here, these ministers had the unenviable task of assessing each department's hastily developed plan to reach some arbitrary cost reduction target that had already been set by the Department of Finance in an effort to make a dent in the federal deficit in time for the 1995 budget.

Whether or not Ottawa was really in the midst of a legitimate fiscal crisis can be debated in hindsight, especially given how quickly Martin ultimately eliminated the deficit. However, there is no doubt that during 1994-95 a crisis environment was created within the government, with power concentrated in the Department of Finance, to ensure that the problem would be tackled in a forthright manner.

While this death by a thousand cuts occupied key ministers, a document more important than Martin's first budget was quietly released under the immodest title of *A New Framework for Economic Policy*. This pithy and lucid eighty-seven-page treatise, written by Peter Nicholson, was eventually labelled the Purple Book. The Purple Book basically did two things. It articulated the intellectual basis for the deficit reduction strategy as an urgent priority for the government. And it identified Canada's lagging productivity as the major source of persistent and stubbornly high unemployment. Conspicuously absent was any mention of Red Book spending initiatives as a way out of the unemployment trap.

In Nicholson's mind, the solution to the economic malaise was to be found in a vigorous deficit reduction program, leading in short order to lower, more stimulative interest rates and a balanced budget. As his Purple Book stated: "A top priority of the government's jobs and growth strategy is therefore to address the factors that are preventing interest rates in Canada from falling to the level warranted by our commitment to low inflation: specifically, this demands *sustained* fiscal discipline, beginning with the government's announced commitment to achieve a deficit to GDP ratio of not more than 3 percent by 1996-97. The ultimate objective is to balance the budget and to significantly reduce the ratio of federal debt to GDP."[10] Nicholson's treatise put the last nail in the coffin of any remaining hopes that Chrétien's crowd would resurrect the old-style Liberal approach to economic management. The analysis bluntly said that fiscal health must be restored through spending cuts, not tax hikes, and it argued for reduced taxes for business,[11] not something Grits or their supporters have usually gotten worked up about.

Besides the fiscal program, Nicholson advocated economic policies such as regulatory and social policy reform, support for R&D, and a more efficient, but not more expensive, education system, to improve productivity, to make Canadian industry more competitive and thereby drive economic growth up and unemployment down. The decline of Canada's growth rate has been almost entirely due to lagging productivity since the 1960s, according to the Purple Book, and slower growth has resulted in rising structural unemployment (what economists refer to as the non-accelerating inflation rate of unemployment or NAIRU). Nicholson argued that the best way governments could get at the persistent part of the unemployment problem was to ensure that more workers got trained in the skills companies wanted, in addition to streamlining government regulations and rooting out disincentives in various income support programs.

This neat little theory reflected the kind of prescriptions that usually come out of think-tanks like the Paris-based OECD and the Toronto-based C.D. Howe Institute. But this thinking wasn't consistent with traditional, or even Red Book, Liberalism, although Nicholson believed his view "articulated a consensus."[12] In fact, the Red Book made only one minor reference to Canada's productivity problems in the manufacturing sector and it certainly shied away from any neocon talk of spending cuts,[13] deregulation, and fixing disincentives in social programs.

Nevertheless, Nicholson managed to convince an initially reluctant Paul Martin that, in the long term, improving productivity was the key to the unemployment problem. As a result, Martin took the Purple Book on board in the hope that it would replace the Red Book as the government's economic policy bible.[14] When all was said and done, Nicholson's emphasis on deficit-fighting pushed aside the Red Book employment policy approach and became the government's raison d'être. In addition to Axworthy's efforts in social policy reform, John Manley, the minister of industry, made some modest efforts to improve Canada's productivity with his *Building a More Innovative Economy* initiative (known as the Orange Book). The deficit, however, was Ottawa's focus, and a full-blown productivity agenda would have to wait at least until Martin cleaned up the fiscal mess.

GREY AND GREEN MAKE EVERYONE BLUE

The pallid grey cover of the 1995 federal budget reflected the distasteful medicine it administered to many Canadians and the chronic sickness of the national economy in the mid-1990s. But it didn't symbolize the bold new approach that this document charted for Canada. In the budget, Martin set forward a truly radical agenda, reflected in its first few pages, which stated, "This Budget will fundamentally reform what the federal government does and how it does it. That reform is *structural* — i.e., it will change permanently the way government operates . . . This will include deep cuts in the *level* of federal program spending — not simply lower spending *growth*, but a substantial reduction in actual dollars spent. This budget secures those savings and confirms the structural changes that will ensure permanent fiscal health."[15]

This was not disposable budget rhetoric like that of the Tories that would be forgotten or jettisoned after the initial blizzard of media coverage. Rather, Martin's statements reflected the new reality of fiscal rectitude in Ottawa that the Liberals had reluctantly embraced a year into their mandate.

There was virtually no significant part of the federal government left untouched by the budget cuts, with the exception of the Department of Indian Affairs and the Equalization program (a program of fiscal transfers from the richer to the poorer provinces).[16] Due to Program Review, all departments and agencies saw their monies cut to fight the deficit, and some were truly transformed by the exercise. For example, Industry

Canada saw most of its business subsidy programs eliminated, including its flagship aerospace support program (although this was reincarnated under another name). Agriculture Canada scrapped the Crow Rate transportation subsidy to grain farmers, which prairie farmers had regarded as an entitlement for decades. And Canada's transport minister in a hurry, Doug Young, probably the most right-wing member of the Chrétien Cabinet, sold off large chunks of his portfolio, such as Canadian National Railways, the Air Navigation System, and the federal airport system. At the end of the day Program Review resulted in about 45,000 permanent federal public service lay-offs.

Another conservative, but probably necessary, innovation in this budget was Martin's so-called contingency fund. During the Mulroney years, Finance gained a terrible reputation for its economic forecasting capabilities, consistently understating deficits by billions of dollars due largely to rosy economic growth forecasts. Martin recognized that his department's forecasting ineptitude could undermine his ability to meet the Red Book deficit target. So to guard against this he decided to build a $3 billion contingency reserve into each year's budget. If the government was wrong in its projections, he could use this money to get closer to the deficit target. The fund would be large enough to take into account forecasting errors on economic growth, revenues, and interest rates, all of which could throw the deficit-fighting agenda off the rails. If the reserve was not used (which it never has been), the $3 billion would go directly to reduce the deficit, not to new spending initiatives.

The most contentious budget change, however, at least from the standpoint of the media, interest groups, and the provinces, was the government's decision to restructure and make deep cuts to transfers to the provinces for what Ottawa spent on health care, post-secondary education, and social assistance. Ottawa paid for these provincially delivered social programs through two separate transfers with distinctly different designs, the Canada Assistance Plan (CAP) and Established Programs Financing (EPF). The CAP was a cost-sharing program with the provinces to pay for social assistance, whereas EPF was a block grant to the provinces for health care and post-secondary education. The budget collapsed these two transfers into one new block fund called the Canada Health and Social Transfer (CHST) and, in the process, cut the overall amount the provinces received from Ottawa by about $6.2 billion.[17] In return, Ottawa would remove many of the conditions it had attached in the past when it allocated this money to the provinces.

In fact, Ottawa killed two birds with one stone. The transfer payment reforms showed the new fiscal austerity that was dominating Ottawa, and also reflected a move to give the provinces more powers. This second and less reported change came as a shock to many, given the Liberals' historic tendency to control things from Ottawa. Now the heirs to the great centralist legacy of Pierre Trudeau were embracing a more neoconservative trend in federal-provincial relations that their rhetorically more decentralist Tory predecessors had rejected a few years earlier.[18]

The 1995 budget was Martin's watershed, his "come hell or high water" program, reflecting his tough statement to the House of Commons Finance Committee a few months previously. The following year's document had a light green, almost grey cover, the true colour of which is difficult to determine. That reflected that budget's ambiguous contents. The third Martin budget did not have a coherent or consistent theme and, like most government budgets, will not be remembered for much of anything. He proposed some very modest spending measures in the areas of tax treatment of children, post-secondary education, youth employment, and technology development. The cornerstone of that year's effort, however, was pension reform.

Canada's public pension system, excluding the Canada Pension Plan (financed by payroll deductions), is expensive, costing the federal government some $20 billion in 1995-96.[19] And the rising number of baby boomers set to retire within the next decade or so will put a big squeeze on the system. So the high priests at Finance figured Ottawa needed to reduce its liabilities. The 1996 budget thus announced that the existing system, comprising Old Age Security, the Guaranteed Income Supplement, Spouses Allowances (all programs created by previous Liberal governments), and the age and pension tax credits, would be replaced by a new income-tested program called the Seniors Benefit. This new benefit actually disguised a modest cost-containment exercise that would better target benefits to those most in need, would be phased in over time, and would not apply to current seniors or anyone over the age of 60. It was a welcome and sensible proposal.

The program was reportedly designed in large part by Ken Battle, a social policy advocate and former head of the National Council of Welfare, a progressive-minded individual and defender of the welfare state if there ever was one. But it represented Martin's boldest gamble in the effort to combat the deficit. Back in 1985 the Mulroney government tried to contain the growth of public pension expenses, but backed down after the well-organized and vocal seniors' lobby made life a political hell for the Tories. Now the Liberals, who had helped lead that attack against the Conservatives' pension reform agenda a decade ago, were walking cautiously down the same path.

Unfortunately, Martin probably announced this necessary change a year too late; had he pushed it in 1995 in the climate of the deficit crisis, it might have flown. By 1996, however, it was increasingly obvious that large deficits would soon be a thing of the past and balanced budgets might even be on the horizon. In a sense Martin had become a victim of his own success.

The Liberals, still smarting from charges that they were imitating the conservative opposition, became increasingly reluctant as time went by to implement the Seniors Benefit, having lost the key fiscal argument for doing so. In 1998, after much angst within the Liberal caucus, criticism from seniors' groups and retirement planning experts, and unfavourable polling numbers, Martin axed the idea.

Consequently, the 1996 budget was basically a stay-the-course document, with few noteworthy initiatives, that remained true to the fiscal prudence proposed in the previous year. There were no hints of an industrial or employment policy agenda as suggested by the Red Book, and Nicholson's productivity call seemed to have been silenced.

These two budgets, 1995 and 1996, marked a watershed in Canada's economic and fiscal policy. For the first time in a generation, Ottawa tackled the deficit in a concerted fashion, and by 1997-98 surpluses were being charted, something that had not been achieved in thirty years. In the process, Ottawa had withdrawn or scaled back from many areas of economic and social policy in which it had been active for decades. The government's accomplishments were monumental when compared to those of its predecessors; few people (including Liberal MPs) thought in 1993 or 1994 that a Liberal government would or could achieve anything like this in such short order.

HOBBLING TOWARDS A NEW AGENDA

Having reached the promised land of a balanced budget, the Chrétien Liberals now looked for a new agenda to run on in 1997. Over the previous three years, the economic policy of the government was one of budget-cutting, support for the Bank of Canada's low inflation policy, and a high-profile international trade strategy, symbolized by the well-publicized Team Canada trade missions led by the prime minister. As the election loomed, the Liberals could point to a record of low inflation and interest rates, stronger economic growth, and, of course, a balanced budget. The unemployment rate, on the other hand, had dropped a couple of points since the Liberals were first elected, but was still unacceptably high. The jobless level hovered around 9 percent, with youth unemployment over 16 percent, indicating that the Liberals' much-touted initiatives in this area were pretty ineffective. Export growth was strong, especially in automobiles, but domestic spending remained weak. The Canadian economy was not reaching the stellar heights of the 1950s or 1960s and was not even living up to its record of the late '80s. On the jobless front, the Liberal economic strategy had not been sufficient by the late 1990s to reduce unemployment to a level close to the country's long-term average.

Martin's 1997 budget, brought down four months before the federal election, demonstrated that Ottawa was staying the fiscal course. But the document also signalled that the Liberals were looking to head in some different directions. There was the usual spending on youth employment programs and small-business financing. The big-ticket items, however, were in post-secondary education and R&D, with the establishment of a Canada Foundation for Innovation to support university research infrastructure. Children also featured prominently, with the announcement that the National Child Benefit had been successfully negotiated with the provinces, the first new federal-provincial social program in decades.

This was quickly followed by Red Book 2, a pale imitator of its predecessor, which failed to articulate anything close to an economic strategy. Its most noteworthy element was a commitment to devote one half of future budget surpluses to new spending and one half to tax cuts and debt reduction, not exactly world-class economic thinking. It was a politically driven formula with no economic rationale that, thankfully, never saw the light of day.

However, the second Red Book and the Liberals' record on the economy were good enough to get them re-elected, albeit with a slimmer majority, and with no small help from Reform and Tory candidates who split the vote in many ridings, especially in Ontario, where the Liberals won all but two seats. Martin stayed on as finance minister, and his first significant initiative of the new mandate was the so-called education budget of 1997, which contained several significant post-secondary education–related measures. Here the big plum was the $2.5 billion Canadian Millennium Scholarships, a pet project of Chrétien himself that some thought would be one of his main legacies. This idea, hastily cobbled together in the Prime Minister's Office with few of its features worked out by the time it was announced, has degenerated into a federal-provincial shouting match with the provinces arguing that it tramples all over their jurisdictions.

Nevertheless, 1998 signalled the beginnings of a new agenda. Instead of more austerity, the government appeared ready to prepare Canadians for the knowledge-based economy through education and modest investments in technology, such as by way of additional support for John Manley's well-received SchoolNet and CANARIE (Canadian Network for the Advancement of Research, Industry and Education) programs.

Tax cuts were also now on the government's radar screen as Martin followed up on successive, but minor, EI premium reductions with an increase in the basic personal income tax exemption for low income Canadians. As well, he eliminated the general surtax — a deficit fighting measure brought in by the Tories — for those earning up to $50,000 a year.

One year later, for the first time since the Liberals took office, the cover of Martin's budget actually had human faces on it rather than bland colours, suggesting that the fixation on the bottom-line number was giving way to a more people-oriented agenda. Previous tough budgets had set the stage for a new era in which Ottawa would have plenty of cash to spend. As a result, Liberals started to announce new spending in health care transfers and medical research and more money for university and business research.[20] More income tax cuts, through the total elimination of the general surtax and further increases in the basic personal exemption, were now affordable. And for the first time in many years the Canadian military, an easy target for cuts, got more money. All of this was done while still balancing the budget and paying down another $3 billion of debt (for a total of around $20 billion debt repayment since the Liberals took office).

BUT WHERE'S THE VISION?

For all their flash, however, the new spending initiatives and tax cuts in 1998-99 were pretty safe stuff for a Liberal finance minister with pockets full of money, a salivating caucus, and grumbling Canadians tired from years of belt-tightening. To be fair, Ottawa was heading in the right direction with its investments in education, innovation, and the information highway, and less emphasis on the old-style and largely ineffective regional and business subsidies. Today, the Liberals, who were never comfortable with a single-minded deficit-fighting agenda, are much more at home with government once again thrashing about in the economy.

Now flush with cash, Chrétien's Liberals are giving everybody a little something to keep them happy. Amidst all the smiles, however, the government has failed to articulate a strategic vision in the key areas that will drive Canada into the twenty-first-century knowledge economy.

The 1999 budget was politically brilliant in appeasing most segments of the Liberal caucus. That is a significant and important challenge for Martin, given his leadership aspirations. At the same time he gave most Canadians a little something to be happy about. But the government demonstrably lacked strategic policy coherence or a clear theme, and, as a result, these changes are unlikely to have significant long-term impact on Canada's economy.

For example, this budget was primarily about health care, with a substantial $11.5 billion in additional transfers to go to the provinces over the next five years. This is exactly what provincial governments, health care professionals, and most other Canadians wanted and indeed demanded from Ottawa. And, being impeccable readers of the public mood, this is what the Liberals delivered. But health care analysts (who do not suffer the conflicts of interests that afflict doctors, nurses, and administrators) are more than a little unconvinced that lack of money is the source of our health care problems, especially when we consider that Canada spends more per capita on health care now, even after the spending restraint of recent years, than most OECD countries. Credible and diverse voices like Ottawa's National Forum on Health, the Simon Fraser University public policy guru John Richards, and the University of British Columbia health economist Bob Evans have all argued that the real problem with our health care system is not lack of money but poor management and anachronistic design features,[21] problems that the provinces must solve since they run the system.

The "health care budget" was in fact more than anything else about politics, about appeasing the Liberal caucus, outflanking federal opposition parties, shutting up interest groups and the premiers, and always the polls.

In a sense, the last two federal budgets, which could have articulated the outlines of a new Liberal agenda based on a coherent economic theory, amount to a missed opportunity for Canada, the first such chance in a generation. Surpluses of the magnitude charted in these years — about $10 billion per year or approximately 1.1 percent of GDP at that time — are rare things in this country's history. The government should therefore have acted upon its good fortune with a dose of a strategic policy direction in mind, especially given that Canada is in the middle of major economic transitions and still faces an appalling unemployment rate even after a few years of strong growth.

During the years from 1947 to 1971, the average federal surplus — taking into account only those years in which there were surpluses — was $500 million, or 1.3 percent of the average GNP in 1985 dollars.[22] Of course, many years during this quarter-century saw deficits as well, and from the early '70s until last year Canadians saw nothing but red ink from the federal government. Realistically, therefore, we can only expect to post annual surpluses on the order of $10 billion if we were to experience another lengthy boom like the one after the Second World War, with an unemployment rate averaging far below the 7.6 percent level at the time of writing. (During the 1947-71 period the unemployment rate averaged under 5 percent.) To say this is unlikely is almost as safe as predicting you will need a block heater during a prairie winter.

Yet a mindset is taking hold in Canada that the big surpluses of the past two years will be the norm for many years to come.[23] History, not to mention common sense, tells us that this is pure wishful thinking. The window of opportunity for the federal government to act in a strategic way with major investments in key areas or tax cuts is probably very narrow. A significant economic slowdown, or even recession, could be right around the corner (B.C. seems to be heading that way now), and is probably no more than a few years off, given global economic instability and the fact that the U.S. expansion has already lasted much longer than anyone ever expected. In the event of a downturn, federal surpluses dry up very quickly as the so-called automatic stabilizers, like unemployment insurance and fiscal stabilization payments, kick in and soak up additional government revenue.[24] During recessions the government has little fiscal room for major new initiatives unless Ottawa is prepared to endure another deficit. And the Canadian public is unlikely to be very enthusiastic about a return to red ink. Deficits are just not on politically in this country any more. Consequently, the big surpluses of the last two years, and the policy opportunities that go along with them, may continue for a year or two more, but not much longer.

WHAT ABOUT THE OPPOSITION?

The Liberals, however, are not the only federal political party to lack strategic policy thinking, or an economic vision. None of the other mainline federal parties has anything to offer in this respect either. The Reform Party is a one-trick pony that advocates major tax cuts and more recently has picked up on the health care theme, largely in a bald appeal for votes. This party is simply not a credible defender of the public health care system, given its rhetoric from 1989 to 1996. One might argue, as Reform has, that a single-minded tax cut agenda does constitute a strategic policy because it would force the government to make tough choices, sacrificing whole areas of spending to finance the cuts. Maybe this case can be made, but we view Reform's tax cut agenda as rooted in both their neoconservative ideology and their populist instincts, not in a thorough analysis of what Canada needs to prosper in the future. Even if Reform's agenda does constitute a new vision, it is the wrong one for Canada. Tax cuts will get us certain things. But they won't take the country much closer to the knowledge-based economy, which must be the core objective of economic and social policy.

As far as the NDP and PCs are concerned, they are still trying to figure out how to survive as viable entities after their trouncings in 1993 and 1997. Parties trying to stay on the map will not be delivering strategic policy direction any time soon. They are too busy fumbling around trying to figure out what it means to be a New Democrat or Progressive Conservative in the twenty-first century to sort out what policies are best for Canada.

BLAME ECONOMICS

The real criticism cannot, however, be laid entirely at the door of the Liberals or any other political party. With the federal deficit war over, we lack an economic theory or role for government, like the one we had in the three decades after the Second World War, that could under-pin a strategic policy agenda that would move the country towards a knowledge economy. The Liberals are therefore merely muddling through, much like a First World War soldier who, having reached one trench, simply stumbles on to the next one, without much of a final objective in mind. Well, while short-sighted, the Chrétien government is not entirely to blame for failing to pursue a longer-term strategy. Now the finger points squarely at the purveyors of the dismal science, economists.

The three previous chapters have outlined the emergence and evo-lution of neoconservative political regimes in Canada, including the swing back towards the policy centre that we are now witnessing. The next part of the book explains the role of economics in the rise and fall of Canada's right wing. Of course, that begs the question, what can a bunch of boring economists tell us about how the new conservatives gained prominence and then fell from favour with the country's electorate?

Political parties need credible policies with which to convince voters to check the correct box at the polling station on election day. That does not mean that a party needs to articulate a detailed, sophisticated platform. Nor does it imply that the general population must immediately run to the popular economic textbook written by Lipsey, Sparks, and Purvis to get a better understanding of the merits of a party's policies.

Even so, a party can bring voters to understand and accept its economic platform over time. A political platform has to reflect what people believe is the proper approach to solving the current problems facing a country, and over the last few decades, economic and financial problems have been paramount concerns in the mind of the electorate. Policies have to be current, address relevant issues, and have some intellectual back-up, which usually means they must be linked in some fashion to a set of economic beliefs or theories.

During the post-war period, two such belief systems — known as Keynesianism, after its founder, the British economist John Maynard Keynes, and monetarism, most commonly associated with the American economist Milton Friedman — have dominated economic policy in Canada and many other industrialized nations. Today, both theories are out of favour with governments and arguably of little help in solving the current economic problems Canada and other advanced nations face.

Governments now face what appears to be an intellectual vacuum. They have yet to latch onto a new set of economic ideas, relevant to the problems of today's global-information economy, from which effective and popular public policies can flow. We will therefore try to outline a new course for governments in this environment, one that is grounded in two relatively new economic theories.

FOUR

PRESENT AT THE CREATION:
KEYNES IN THE
MODERN WORLD

"The modern government budget must be the balance wheel of the economy."[1]

ROBERT BRYCE: KEYNES COMES TO CANADA

Shove a group of well-educated Canadians into a room and ask this question: Who is Robert Bryce? More than likely, you will get some pained looks, embarrassed shuffling of feet, and blank stares for your troubles. Yet Robert Bryce was one of the most influential figures in post-war Ottawa and the man who brought the ideas of the great British economist John Maynard Keynes to Canada.

Born in 1910 and raised in Toronto's affluent Rosedale district, Bryce wanted to be an engineer just like his father, and with this goal in mind he headed to the University of Toronto. Then the Depression hit and Bryce decided that plumbing the depths of the global economy held more interest than an engineer's slide rule. That about-face changed the course of his life as well as that of Canadian public policy for the next forty years.

For the best and brightest of Bryce's generation who were interested in cutting-edge economics, the place to study was the University of Cambridge under Keynes. And that's where Bryce wanted to go. So despite a lack of formal training in economics, he used his grades and raw intellect to secure himself a spot in the Cambridge graduate economics program in 1932, just when Keynes's power and influence were in the ascendancy both in academia and government.

In the previous decade Keynes had completed an impressive stint in the British government, including a key role in the Versailles Treaty negotiations during which, ever the iconoclast, he argued against the hugely popular idea of saddling Germany with massive war reparations as punishment for starting the First World War. Unfortunately, his reasoning was way ahead of its time and his views were summarily rejected by the British government and her allies in favour of a strategy of bankrupting the vanquished powers to cripple their war machine, which was a major cause of the rise of Hitler and ultimately the Second World War.

As a consequence, Keynes left the government to write what became a dissonant, important, and surprisingly popular book on the Versailles treaty, *The Economic Consequences of the Peace*. Cambridge University then beckoned, and from there in the 1920s Keynes made significant contributions to the understanding of the role of money in the economy, establishing himself as a leading monetary economist (although forty years later monetary theories would take the lead in displacing the ideas for which Keynes is most famous).

At the time of Bryce's arrival, Keynes's lectures were largely devoted to outlining a new book he was completing. It was called *The General Theory of Employment, Interest, and Money* and was published in 1936, turning the economics discipline (and ultimately the agenda of many governments around the world) on its head. Bryce was one of the few Canadians present at both the conception and birth of *The General Theory*, and this early exposure led him years later to preach the new economic gospel on this side of the Atlantic Ocean.

The General Theory articulated a radical argument for an academic book at a time when polite intellectual discussions were the norm. Keynes wanted to solve the chronic unemployment problem of the 1930s, but he concluded that conventional economic thinking did not provide the answers. Consequently, he developed a new theory, launching a direct attack on the basic premises of what he called classical economics, ideas that had held sway since the time of Adam Smith in the eighteenth century.

Smith held that an invisible hand in the market guided self-interested consumers towards the best outcome for society. Classical economists maintained that an economy would find equilibrium between supply and demand through the natural workings of the market. If government and societal institutions set the conditions for an unfettered market to exist, wages and prices would adjust quickly to changes in demand, resulting in equilibrium, or a situation where what was demanded would equal what was supplied and full employment would result. In the classical world there would really be no such thing as economic policy because markets would clear naturally by their own volition. The role of government (as distinct from the monetary authority) would be limited to setting the legal framework within which markets would operate.

Keynes's observation of economic conditions in Britain during the Depression led him to question this doctrine, mainly because it appeared to him that demand and supply were indeed meeting, but at unacceptable levels of unemployment. As a result, Keynes set out to find a new theory to explain this phenomenon and offer some way out of the malaise. The fruit of his endeavours was *The General Theory*, a virtually impenetrable book but nevertheless a bold attempt at theory-building and policy prescription, which was subsequently simplified (and probably distorted) and labelled Keynesianism.

Boiled down to its essence, *The General Theory* argued that the stagnation of the Depression was attributable to insufficient demand in the economy and price-wage deflation. Keynes believed that high unemployment was stifling spending and business investment, causing a vicious circle leading to more unemployment, thereby further weakening purchasing power and capital spending. During these years wages did not seem to fall in keeping with declining demand as quickly as classical theory would predict, leading Keynes to conclude that wages were "sticky" downwards. This was due in part to the fact that eighteenth and nineteenth century economists had not foreseen the rise of trade union power, which helped keep wages up even when demand was down.

Keynes also thought the British monetary authority's preoccupation with inflation was totally misplaced and that interest rates had risen too high, resulting in deflation or falling prices, which even for traditional thinkers is generally regarded as worse than inflation.

The central message of *The General Theory* was that an economy can be at equilibrium, where available supply meets available demand, at less than full employment, a conclusion that was based on a short-term examination of the economy. The classical theory emphasized the long-term, in which such a situation was said to be impossible. Keynes, in contrast, showed his monumental self-confidence and contempt for the older ideas by writing his most famous line: "In the long run we are all dead."

Keynes's *General Theory* argued that the relationship between savings and investment was key to economic growth, and when the private sector failed to close the gap between them, government policy could make up the difference. But he did not agree with the conventional wisdom of that time, which also holds sway today, that the key to investment decisions was monetary policy or changes in interest rate levels. Rather, Keynes thought economies could fall into what he called "liquidity traps," in which economic conditions, like those during the Depression, get so bad that people see few benefits in borrowing money for investing, even at very low rates of interest. (This is probably the situation in Japan today, where, despite interest rates approaching zero, the economy remains stagnant.)

Consequently, England's great monetary theorist decided that the fiscal side of the economy provided the answer to insufficient investment, and hence to unemployment. Thus he carved out a positive role for government, not just for central banks, in managing economies: what came to be known as demand management, a heresy to classical economists.

Under this new doctrine demand could be stimulated and maintained by governments through the use of tax cuts and spending programs, particularly universal income security programs. This was the first solid macroeconomic rationale for the building of a welfare state. If the economy was underperforming, the government should step in by boosting public expenditures or cutting taxes. And, even further at odds with the classical crowd, running deficits was not only acceptable but preferable to balanced budgets during recessions.

The mind of the young Bryce when he arrived at Cambridge was not cluttered or indoctrinated with the classical shibboleths that *The General Theory* assaulted. Hence he accepted these radical ideas probably more readily than his classmates, who had been schooled for several years in the conventional ideas.[2] But for young idealists in search of a way out of the prevailing global economic malaise, the new thinking was intuitively persuasive and offered an optimistic future in the midst of the most pessimistic period of the twentieth century.

Bryce thus became a disciple of the great man,[3] joining the Cambridge Political Economy Club, where Keynes had held court since 1909 over intimate dinners. Membership in this elite group was by invitation only, consisting of Keynes's closest colleagues, graduate students, and a few of the brightest undergraduates.[4] Bryce began his doctoral dissertation under Keynes, although he abandoned this work in favour of a career in government back in Canada. Nevertheless, Bryce wrote one of the first papers explaining *The General Theory* even before the book's publication.

Keynes was impressed with the Canadian's understanding of his emerging doctrine, and, as a result, Bryce became a proselytizer, attempting to convert the London School of Economics and Harvard economics faculties and students to the new gospel. Bryce's lecture notes from 1932 to 1935 are regarded as important sources on Keynes's thinking before his book was published, illustrating Bryce's importance to the dissemination and understanding of Keynesianism.

After two years at Harvard, Bryce returned to Canada and almost immediately came to the attention of the federal deputy minister of finance, W. Clifford Clark (who is now recognized at the Department of Finance through the annual appointment of the Clifford Clark Visiting Economist, a senior adviser to the minister of finance and the position that Peter Nicholson held in 1994-95). Before joining the department, Clark had worked as an academic and a business economist, and was an early proponent of a Canadian central bank. He did not know much about Keynes's theories, however, until Bryce came along. Clark persuaded him to join Finance in 1938 and from then on Bryce's star soared. He was promoted to assistant deputy minister and secretary to the Treasury Board at the tender age of thirty-seven, a position he held from 1947 to 1954.

In the federal civil service, Bryce went beyond being an intellectual proponent of demand management to become a committed practitioner of the government stimulus approach to economic policy. He was the driving force behind Ottawa's adoption of Keynes's ideas, giving them the stranglehold on the federal government over the next thirty years. When Bryce left Finance for the Privy Council Office in 1954, Keynesianism had pushed out classical economics as the orthodoxy in Ottawa. Any politician, bureaucrat, or academic who wanted to make his mark had to promote some version of this theory. From his vantage point as clerk of the Privy Council from 1954 to 1963, the head of the federal public service and senior adviser to the prime minister, Bryce presided over a federal bureaucracy that he, more than anyone else, had pushed along the Keynesian path. In 1963, Bryce returned to Finance as deputy minister at the request of the newly elected prime minister, Lester Pearson, who wanted Canada's foremost Keynesian at the helm. Bryce's presence in the most senior ranks of the federal government throughout the post-war period ensured the theories he learned at Cambridge during the early 1930s were the pre-eminent influence over the policies of both Liberal and Conservative administrations into the 1970s.

KEYNESIANISM AT WORK

Canada's first modest foray into demand management, indeed perhaps the first concerted attempt at Keynesian policy anywhere in the world, was the 1939 federal budget. It is no coincidence that this budget was the first one Bryce worked on. Previously the idea of government spending to stimulate the economy was anathema. As Ian Drummond notes in his study of Canadian economic history for the MacDonald Royal Commission, before the Second World War Canadian governments did not manipulate taxing and spending to balance macroeconomic or other objectives. What they did do was undertake what today would be called megaprojects, "blithely ignoring" their overall economic impacts.[5]

During the Depression, Canada, like Keynes's Britain, suffered deflation and unemployment that reached 20 percent. In the early 1930s, wholesale farm prices dropped by more than half at a time when agriculture was still a huge part of the Canadian economy. Canada's GNP accordingly declined by 43 percent between 1929 and 1933.[6] The Conservative government of R.B. Bennett, elected in 1931, dealt with this crisis by following the classical approach of tight fiscal and monetary policy. The only other efforts his government made to correct the underlying economic problems were initiatives to protect certain sectors of the Canadian economy from foreign competition while simultaneously trying to pry open foreign markets for Canadian exports. This hands-off approach during desperate economic times failed miserably and Bennett paid the ultimate political price when his government was defeated four years later.

The Liberals under Mackenzie King then took over, but followed a similar economic plan to their predecessors, with the primary goal being a balanced budget and increased trade. In the 1936 budget speech, King's finance minister, Charles Dunning, stated that this approach would "contribute more effectively to the solution of the problems of unemployment and depression than any other single thing that governments can do."[7] Fortunately for King, the U.S. economy began to recover during the middle part of the decade due, in part, to President Franklin Roosevelt's policies, some of which had a distinctly Keynesian flavour. And the Canadian economy was pulled along for the ride.[8]

By 1938, the relevance of Keynes's analysis had been recognized in Canada by the National Employment Commission, which endorsed a mild form of demand stimulus. And by 1939 Dunning had abandoned classical policies in favour of a Keynesian approach. This was reflected in a statement in the House of Commons: "In these days, if the people as a whole, and business in particular, will not spend, government must."[9]

The Second World War hit in September of that year, requiring massive public spending and manpower, thereby effectively ending the Depression. The pump-priming approach to economic management was practised *de facto* during that conflict. But the Keynesian revolution in Canadian policy-making really began in the post-war period.

Just before the end of the war, the federal government tabled a policy statement in Parliament called *Employment and Income*, which signalled the new direction upon which the King government was about to embark. This document built upon the government's 1943 *Report on Social Security for Canada* (the Marsh Report), which laid out the rationale and policies for a Canadian welfare state. *Employment and Income* also pointed out the importance of newly established income security programs, such as unemployment insurance and family allowances, not only to the financial well-being of Canadians, but to the overall health of the Canadian economy.[10]

Ottawa was building a case for more government involvement in the workings of the marketplace due to a legitimate fear that the mass unemployment of the Depression would return once the war production machine wound down. Consequently, the core of the government's post-war agenda became fighting the unemployment that was feared would result from demobilization. The government's effort was Keynesianism in action: a macroeconomic policy designed specifically to maintain high levels of employment through government spending and intervention in the economy. Ottawa could not have summarized Keynesianism better than in its own clarion call: "The government will be prepared, in periods when unemployment threatens, to incur the deficits and increases in the national debt resulting from its employment and income policy."[11] As J. Harvey Perry noted, "From 1945 on the annual budget, once devoted to largely an accounting of the position of the treasury, became as much an economic as a fiscal document."[12] Government spending had become a deliberately used instrument in Canada's economy. This new and expensive agenda was pursued even though, as a result of the war, the federal government was saddled with the largest public debt in Canadian history.

Keynes's economic theories, however, cannot get all the credit for this new approach to economic management and the social and industrial policies that flowed from it. There were other equally important political and policy imperatives that influenced these initiatives at least as much as *The General Theory*.[13] But Keynes's theory provided the underlying macroeconomic rationale.

TURNING ON THE TAP

Ottawa's new spending agenda consisted of unemployment insurance, universal income security programs such as family allowances and old age pensions, transfers to provinces for social assistance and post-secondary education, public housing initiatives, infrastructure projects, such as the St. Lawrence Seaway, the establishment of numerous federal Crown corporations like Air Canada, and extensive regional development programs. These initiatives took many years to develop, culminating with the Pearson government's ambitious agenda, which included the Canada Assistance Plan, a 50-50 cost-sharing transfer program to provinces to support social assistance ("welfare"), the

Guaranteed Income Supplement for the elderly, and universal health care. The cumulative cost of these initiatives was high, and their existence was a major reason for federal deficits during many of the post-war years.

For example, in 1966 the federal government was spending about $1.4 billion per year on old age pensions and the Guaranteed Income Supplement alone. And by 1983 this number leaped to almost $9.5 billion. Similarly, family allowance payments cost Ottawa half a billion dollars in the mid-'60s, but $2.2 billion by 1983.[14] From 1947 to 1979 real government expenditure on goods and services, after subtracting the effects of inflation, rose on average 5.5 percent per annum. During the same period, real private consumption increased by only 4.9 percent a year.

Throughout this era, unemployment, the government's primary concern, remained very low. It was 3.4 percent in 1966, a full twenty years after the government adopted the Keynesian approach. Consequently, in spite of the costs, these programs largely survived intact until the fiscal problems of the late '80s and early '90s. This was partly because the public regarded many of them as entitlements and basic elements of a just society. But Ottawa also thought the programs provided positive long-term benefits to the economy that outweighed their negative short-term fiscal impact. In short, they were regarded as economic assets more than fiscal drags.

Unfortunately there was trouble on the horizon in Canada. The first signs of fiscal problems began to emerge in the late '50s when Ottawa posted annual deficits in the hundreds of millions. In the next decade deficits and surpluses alternated, but shortfalls were tolerated because they seemed to be a way of keeping unemployment down and growth up. From 1948 to 1972, nominal GDP growth averaged 8.6 percent.[15] And the average jobless rate during the period was under 5 percent, which compared more than favourably to the 20 percent rate of 1933. To many Canadians, and certainly to the politicians, the economic boom and the unprecedented prosperity experienced during this period seemed to be connected to government policy. Many other advanced industrial democracies likewise jumped on the Keynesian bandwagon during these years, with similar good results.

By the early 1960s, the interventionist approach to economic management had become so entrenched in Ottawa that it even managed to survive an embarrassing public confrontation between James Coyne, governor of the Bank of Canada, and the Diefenbaker government. Coyne started a crisis in 1961 by publicly opposing the government's lax fiscal policy. In the end, instead of following the tougher line prescribed by the irksome Coyne, Diefenbaker dumped the governor, a course of action virtually unthinkable today. This episode symbolized the government's still strong commitment to the Keynesian path fully fifteen years after Ottawa began its trek down this road. The dominance of the Keynesian doctrine was clearly evident in Canada and throughout the world by the late 1960s when even conservatives like Richard Nixon had to concede that "we are all Keynesians now."[16]

KEYNES FALLS FROM GRACE

Cracks in this longstanding orthodoxy, however, began to show in the 1970s. In the wake of the first oil crisis in 1973, a major supply shock boosted inflation and unemployment simultaneously throughout the industrialized world, something that many mainstream economists had thought impossible. This phenomenon was known as stagflation. Federal deficits, which had been small or non-existent over the past twenty years, began to balloon, breaking the psychologically important $10 billion mark in 1980. More importantly, the unemployment rate jumped to more than 7 percent in 1976 for the first time since the Depression, and worse still, headed up to 8.1 percent in 1977 and 8.4 percent in 1978.[17] Talk began to emerge of a natural or structural rate of unemployment that governments could do little about without driving up inflation further. Consumer and business confidence was low and voters were blaming elected officials.

When governments of the day turned to the Keynes tool box to fix these problems they found to their consternation that it was empty. His theory was designed for a different time and circumstance, when deflation was the problem. Now inflation was ravaging the economy and the post-war approach seemed to offer few answers, perhaps even exacerbate the situation by adding more fuel to the inflation fire, in the form of higher government spending. Governments around the world appeared helpless to deal with the core economic problems they faced, as unemployment, inflation, and deficits spiralled upward in this period.

By 1980, Canada was rocked by another recession, partly the result of a second oil crisis. In an effort to combat an inflation rate of 12.5 percent, the highest in post-war Canada, the central bank boosted interest rates to unprecedented levels, cracking 20 percent in 1981. To put this in perspective, Canadian interest rates had never exceeded 7.5 percent until 1978.[18] In 1982, the federal budget deficit broke through the $20 billion ceiling, double what it had been just two years before, while real GDP growth was -4.4 percent. In recognition that even 20 percent interest rates were not enough to dampen double-digit inflation, Allan MacEachen, the finance minister, instituted the "6 and 5" restraint program in his 1982 budget. This initiative held wage and price increases to 6 percent in 1982 and 5 percent in 1983 in the federal public sector. The government also attempted to convince the broader public and private sectors to follow suit. These unprecedented measures helped bring inflation down to 5.8 percent in 1983 (an intolerable level by today's standards), but at considerable cost. Unemployment shot up to 11.9 percent that year.[19] It was abundantly evident that Canada, and indeed the entire industrial world, was in the midst of an economic calamity not seen since the Depression. And governments appeared to have neither the policies nor the theory to address the situation.

KEYNES IS DEAD, AT LEAST FOR NOW

The economic crisis of the 1970s and early 1980s spelled the end of the Keynesian consensus in Canada and throughout the industrialized world. In the 1980s, the American conservative intellectual Irving Kristol was able to proudly pronounce Keynes dead. At the same time a conservative economic theory called monetarism, claiming to be the panacea for all economic ills, was about to take over. This approach was not new; indeed, monetarism was part of the pre-Keynes ortho-doxy that the great man had taken pleasure in assaulting. However, by the late 1970s, monetarism had taken on a new life, spearheaded internationally by the University of Chicago academic Milton Friedman, who, like Keynes, became one of the most influential economists of the twentieth century.

Friedman came from a totally different perspective about the role of government in the economy. Nevertheless, his thinking would prove as influential on governments for the next decade as Keynesianism had been on those of the preceding forty years. But monetarism would also eventually run its course, as governments gradually came to realize that this doctrine was no better at solving the problem of ever-rising levels of unemployment than its predecessor had been.

FIVE

MONETARISTS AS
BOMB THROWERS

CANADA HITS THE WALL

Canada's devotion to the doctrine of John Maynard Keynes, which had wavered since the beginning of the 1970s, came to a crashing if perhaps temporary end on Thanksgiving night 1975, when Prime Minister Pierre Trudeau announced on national television that his government was introducing a plan for wage and price controls.

Already that September the finance minister, John Turner, had resigned from the Liberal government, unable to secure a voluntary agreement between business and labour to restrain their wage and price demands. A month later, Canadian firms found themselves in a worse position, forced to justify their prices before a new creation, the Anti-Inflation Board, and workers were subject to a set ceiling on pay hikes.

Trudeau and his cabinet made this drastic move as a way of dealing with the country's soaring inflation rate. By doing so, however, they also relegated notions of tinkering with taxes and spending to buoy national demand, the essence of political Keynesianism, to university textbooks and academic conferences.

Fewer people now believed that the indirect approach to controlling prices would work. Instead, the Trudeau government opted for a more muscular style of policy-making. Ottawa figured, if you do not have any obvious answer to the present problem, set the rules for the market-place directly. At least voters might give you points for trying.

That interpretation, however, is putting the best face on a bad situation. In fact, Trudeau's implementation of economic controls was a major retreat for his government. The Liberals eventually would put together such interventionist initiatives as the National Energy Program and the Foreign Investment Review Agency, as well as create Crown corporations, such as Petro-Canada. But never again would the Grits attempt to battle unemployment to the exclusion of other economic goals.

In fact, the country's ability to create jobs would forever become a residual policy, something that happened after Ottawa tamed inflation or shored up a sinking dollar.

FLIPPING FASTER THAN A LANDED TROUT

The charismatic Trudeau had just turned his minority government into a majority one in the federal election of 1974 by beating the Progressive Conservative leader, Robert Stanfield. During the campaign, he success-fully ridiculed the plodding Tory leader's suggestion of state intervention to slow the rate of price increases. "Zap. You're frozen" became one of the Liberal leader's key punchlines in his election speeches.

Making fun of the slow Stanfield was easy for the verbally nimble Trudeau. Unfortunately, in terms of economic policy, he had little else up his sleeve during that campaign besides glib one-liners. Inflation continued to rise unabated. And Ottawa was powerless to stop it. So, sixteen months later, there sat Trudeau, "wearing his heavy-duty, navy-blue crisis suit,"[1] telling Canadians that they were indeed frozen economically, only by a Liberal regime. Trudeau, never a heavyweight in economic matters, broke his word to voters, mainly because Canada's economic problems had reached a point at which the politicians and the civil servants lost confidence in traditional solutions.

Tommy Shoyama, the well-respected, consensus-building deputy minister of finance, became the point man in the bureaucratic effort after the election to change Trudeau's mind regarding wage and price controls. Shoyama argued that consumers, workers, and businesses would not rein in their behaviour until Ottawa sent a strong signal that it was serious about stopping inflation. People and companies would refuse to curtail excessive wage and price demands unless the government showed it was willing to reinforce tough talk with decisive action. Such a policy was critical if the Liberals were to break the self-fulfilling prophecy of inflation and lower everyone's expectations for continuously rising prices.

WHY WHAT YOU THINK MATTERS

Here's the economic problem Ottawa faced. If people always believe prices are heading skywards, they will adjust their own demands in a heavenly direction in response. If you think prices are going to be 5 percent higher next year compared to the current twelve months, you will ask for a wage increase to cover that loss in spending power. In your contract demands, you will request an "inflation premium," plus what you expect as a reward for your improved performance.

Of course, the company for whom you toil will need to earn extra cash to cover the higher wages. In addition, management may expect the prices for other things the firm needs to make its products, such as raw materials and energy, to rise next year. Thus, instead of boosting prices a bit to cover new wage demands, the firm might wind up hiking what it charges consumers by an even larger amount to pay for all these higher input costs.

In the middle '70s, economists argued that Ottawa and the central bank needed somehow to lower these spiralling expectations among Canadians if the government ever wanted to slow the rising rate of inflation. As long as people believed the federal government was willing to tolerate higher prices, they would be unlikely to change their behaviour.

In a Keynesian world, expectations are not central to halting inflation. It is mainly a matter of printing less money, hiking taxes, or cutting public spending. In these three cases, demand for goods and services in the economy should fall in response, relieving the pressure on producers to pay higher wages and retailers to continuously raise their final prices.

Governments had generally interpreted Keynesianism to mean increasing or decreasing the amount of public spending to adjust the level of demand in an economy. By the mid-1970s, however, many politicians and economists were losing faith in these long-standing answers in the face of Canada's growing inflation and unemployment crisis.

Between 1965 and 1969, Canada's national jobless figure averaged 4.2 percent, an improvement over the previous five years, but in line with the country's post-war experience. During the next half-decade, however, annual unemployment averaged 5.9 percent, a jump of 40 percent from the previous five years. And that was only the beginning. Canada's jobless level would peak at 8.3 percent in 1979 and average 7.6 percent over the second half of the decade.[2]

Keynes's theories were supposed to deal with rising unemployment through higher public spending. His supporters argued joblessness was a result of consumers not buying enough of the goods and services that businesses produced. When the unemployment rate was very high, government needed to step in and spend the cash that Canadians were hoarding. Thus, a deficit became an economic virtue, keeping afloat an economy that would otherwise stagnate.

(Lest one think that Keynes's theory has no application these days, many people argue that Japan is caught in a classic liquidity trap. No matter how far the government cuts interest rates, no one is interested in borrowing money. As a result, many conservative voices, such as *The Economist* magazine, argue that Japan needs to hike public spending as one part of a solution to the country's lack of economic growth.)

Predictably, in the 1970s, Ottawa spent more as Canada's unemployment rate rose to address the problem. In 1970, the government had expenditures of $15.7 billion. By 1979, that figure had soared to $53.4 billion, a jump of almost two-and-one-half times.

At this point, however, the script diverges. Instead of falling, Canada's unemployment rate kept rising, in spite of higher public spending. At the same time as the jobless figures were defying gravity, inflation also began soaring skywards.

In 1975, the year Trudeau brought in wage and price controls, inflation stood at 10.8 percent, a marginal drop from 10.9 percent one year earlier. But contrast that figure with the 1971 rate of 2.9 percent and it is obvious why alarm bells were going off in official circles about the country's inflation level. At this rate, Canada could face 20 percent inflation by the end of the decade.[3]

The appearance of the twin problems of higher unemployment and inflation had Keynes's followers scratching their heads. After all, joblessness and prices were not supposed to increase at the same time.

One certainty of the much-touted Phillips Curve was that prices would remain steady in the face of rising unemployment. With such a large number of Canadians without work, Ottawa should have at least been confident that inflation would remain stable.

Unfortunately, in Canada and many other countries, both variables were now heading north, a trend that governments throughout the industrialized world seemed powerless to halt, especially given the policy solutions at hand.

OTTAWA CROSSES ITS FINGERS

Faced with rising inflation and growing skepticism among economists on how to handle the problem, Shoyama's arguments about inflationary expectations and the belief that doing something — anything — was better than sitting on your hands carried the day. Wage and price controls became a Canadian reality.

The country's experiment with these controls lasted three years and managed to reduce the rate of price increases to 8.8 percent in 1978, down from 10.8 percent in 1975. Ottawa had always argued that its anti-inflation program was meant to give the economy a "breathing space" during which the various groups could recognize the necessity of moderating their wage and price demands.[4] The government did not believe that a system of permanent controls was worthwhile. So, in April 1978, Ottawa announced that it would phase out the price control system that year.

Rising inflation, not increasing unemployment, now became the main target of government policy. Ottawa made that choice partly because it believed the traditional solution of turning on the spending spigot was not reducing joblessness and, in fact, might be worsening inflation. Besides, many analysts felt that inflation had become the country's biggest economic problem, one that the government had the power to solve.

Ian Macdonald, the president of York University, said at the time that Canadians could accept the medicine of wage and price controls or catch a "serious illness that might be terminal."[5]

Ottawa was not yet ready to pursue an alternative strategy of cranking up interest rates to the point of driving unemployment to the levels necessary to halt inflation. Still, the government had moved far away from the idea that unemployment, not inflation, was its main concern. As one observer noted subsequently, "While there was no formal abandonment of the employment objective, by 1975 it was clear that 'something' had changed. The employment objective had obviously lost its political and moral resonance, and faith in the Keynesian tools had diminished."[6]

In fact, government now looked upon inflation as a sign of higher unemployment to come, a scenario that would have been bizarre to economists a generation earlier.

As Liberal finance minister Donald Macdonald stated in 1976: "If we fail to bring the rate of inflation down, we will also fail in our efforts to achieve sustained reductions in the level of unemployment."[7]

In Canada and in other countries that experienced similar economic woes, it seemed Keynes had a new bedmate, one ready to steal all the covers. And, unlike the sophisticated Keynes, Milton Friedman was abrasive and hard-hitting. There would be no more Mr. Nice Guy in economic policy.

ENTER FRIEDMAN

Anyone who knew of the acerbic University of Chicago economics professor in the 1970s likely recognized him from his public battles with John Kenneth Galbraith, a Canadian-born Harvard professor.

The lanky Galbraith argued for many years that the structure of the industrial economy had changed, leading to a fundamental shift in how governments should deal with prices, growth, and unemployment. Elected officials and bureaucrats needed to be more active in how they regulated this kind of economy, to prevent bad behaviour by big unions and even bigger companies. With his theories, the Elgin County, Ontario, native represented the latest in the line of institutional economists like Thorstein Veblen, thinkers who believed how companies and governments operated could determine how the economy as a whole developed.

Friedman followed another longstanding strand of economic thought, only his dated from John Stuart Mill in the nineteenth century and emphasized the monetary side of the economy.

In the 1960s, while Galbraith was required bedtime reading for any aspiring politician, Friedman was a curiosity, interesting but ultimately out of step with current thinking. That meant politicians and public policy types generally ignored him. After all, hadn't governments already found the key to eliminating their economic woes through Keynes?

As the 1970s progressed, however, problems once believed to have been banished to the history books returned with a vengeance. Everyone was looking for ways to deal with rising inflation and unemployment. And Friedman had a new answer in an old theory.

Throughout most of his career, Friedman had flogged the virtues of stable money as the key to a nation's economic health. He was not talking about a gold-backed currency, the policy people usually associated with this term, but to a bit of the economy few politicians and fewer voters knew much about: the money supply.

In this case, Friedman focused on the amount of dollars that physically pass from hand to hand as well as in certain kinds of bank accounts, such as non-interest-bearing demand deposits, that act like money in pocket. He was using a theory made famous by the U.S.

economist Irving Fisher in the early part of the twentieth century to punch holes in prevailing liberal economic thinking.

Fisher and Alfred Marshall were two of the biggest names in economics in the years before Keynes. Both men promoted the use of market forces as the best regulator of economic activity. In the eyes of these two giants, businesses, workers, and consumers, acting in their own best interests, would guarantee the best results for the entire economy. Fisher for one made no bones about his disdain for government interference in this sphere.[8]

MONETARY BASICS

With his monetary theory, Fisher figured all economic activity could fit into a four-variable equation: $MV = PQ$. The PQ refers to gross domestic product (GDP) in current dollars, that is, without adjusting for inflation. The P is the general price level of the economy while the Q is shorthand for the actual amount of goods and services produced. The left-hand side of the equation represents the money side of the economy. M stands for the amount of cash (with a few extras) that is floating around the country at any one time. V refers to its velocity or the number of times that this money changes hands in a particular period, say, a year.

To economists, this equation is almost a truism. The right-hand side presents what a country produces and the left-hand side how people and businesses pay for that same stuff. There was no controversy among economists so far.

But the equation gets trickier when you add in a simple assumption. Suppose you pick a short time frame like a month. The amount of goods and services that an economy can produce during that period is unlikely to change. After all, businesses are already set up to produce a certain amount. Nothing in the next few days or weeks is likely to change that.

Similarly, the number of times money changes hands — V in the equation — is probably not going to increase or drop during the month beyond a set amount. So, consider this figure fixed as well.

That leaves the price level, P, and the money supply, M, as the only things in this simple math problem that can change in value over a short period. Now, remember the central bank controls the money supply through interest rates or by printing new coin and bills. Thus, in Fisher's world, increasing or decreasing the amount of money travelling throughout the economy boosts or reduces the price level. In its starkest form, the theory says that the growth in the country's money supply dictates its rate of price increases.[9]

Thus, only the money supply can affect inflation. Print a lot of money and expect prices to jump. Churn out less cash and you should see inflation fall.

Friedman believed that keeping a lid on how much cash was in circulation throughout an economy was the crucial, if not the only, variable dictating the level of inflation in the country. Most people know the crude version of this theory as monetarism.

Friedman and his fellow-travellers believed that the money supply should only expand by an amount equal to how fast the value of the country's economy, or GDP, increases. If a government increases the amount of cash in circulation faster than the rate of economic growth, overall employment will not rise. Friedman argued that such policies would lead to more money flowing throughout the economy chasing the same amount of goods and service as before. And that situation would lead to higher inflation.

The only way to improve a country's job situation was by allowing markets to work in a more unencumbered way by restricting unions, and by eliminating minimum wages and other well-intended, but wrong-headed, liberal machinations. Following Keynes was a prescription for more economic problems, according to Friedman.

These views were not popular with many mainstream voters twenty-five years ago. Canadians were less than thrilled with the idea of eliminating obvious benefits for working men and women and getting rid of rules that kept companies within the bounds of decent behaviour. It smacked of a kind of hair-shirt public policy, in which you were only better off by enduring some sort of painful ordeal.

These types of policies were designed to remove government from the economic equation as much as possible. Elected officials, according to this school of thought, had very little to do with the proper functioning of an economy and were best not involved at all.

MONETARISM CREEPS NORTH

While the market freedom theology may have fallen on deaf ears among politicians, the monetarist message of tight money was finding an audience at the Bank of Canada. During the 1970s, Gerald Bouey, the governor of the Bank of Canada, began making speeches in which he endorsed the idea of using monetary aggregates to set economic policy.

A monetary aggregate is a fancy way of describing how much currency is in circulation. Different monikers, such as M1 all the way to M3, were used to make increasingly comprehensive measurements of a country's money supply. By reading these figures properly, these central bankers should be able to tell by these separate instruments whether and by how much certain economic measurements, like GDP, would increase.

Monetarists wanted Bouey to restrict the money growth to stay in line with the desired level of inflation. So, to bring the rate of price increases down to three or four percent from 10 percent, a government or central bank needed to keep the growth in M1 equal to the lower figure.

Keynesianism always implied that an economy could get an easy ride to prosperity. You simply borrowed or printed more money and everyone would have a job. But the puritans who inhabited the monetarist camp said the only free lunch is one past the due date on that lunch's packaging. An economy prospers when its employees work harder and its owners make the right investment decisions, not when a government finds another gullible banker from whom to borrow or cranks up the money presses.

How much Bouey bought the monetarist argument has always been a question. Tired of past failures through fine-tuning interest rates, the taciturn governor was willing to try a monetary-based theory to get inflation under some control.

After all, between 1971 and 1975, the growth of M1 averaged 12.9 percent annually and inflation accelerated from 2.9 percent in 1971 to 10.8 percent four years later. Even if there was not a direct correlation between the expansion of these two figures, there had to be some connection. Since everything else had failed, ratcheting down money supply growth was worth a try.

Politically, though, Bouey had a big problem. Besides keeping the value of the currency high and the rate of price hikes low, the Bank of Canada has the mandate "generally to promote the economic and financial welfare of Canada."[10] Throwing crowds of unemployed Canadians on the streets, implicitly the outcome of restricting monetary growth in a bid to smash inflation, would not be considered fulfilling that portion of the Bank's function.

In 1975, Bouey and the officials at the Bank devised a nicely

Canadian solution to the debate about whether to be hard-hearted or soft-headed. Rather than turning the monetary tap off completely, Bouey chose to limit money supply growth, as defined by M1, to a target band, with the goal of reducing the range over time. The Bank's plan, known as gradualism, held the promise of lowering inflation without killing growth in the economy.

Between 1975 and 1981, the Bank tried to corral the inflation horse by lowering the rate of money growth, specifically by controlling the expansion of M1, one of the most restricted monetary measures. Bouey's bank did hit its monetary targets.

TABLE 1: M1 GROWTH BETWEEN 1975 AND 1981[11]

PERIOD	M1 TARGET	ACTUAL AVERAGE
May '75 to March '76	10–15% per year	10.7%
March '76 to June '77	8–12	8.9
June '77 to June '78	7–11	8.5
June '78 to Jan. '80	6–10	7.6
Jan. '80 to Feb. '81	5–9	6.5

As well, the Bank of Canada started announcing its targets in advance, giving consumers, workers, and businesses a chance to get their inflationary expectations in line with the government's plan, a prerequisite for effective monetary policy.

Unfortunately, the country's rate of inflation decided not to play along with the theory. Canadians should have seen the rate of price hikes decrease in line with the lower M1 growth. The reduction should have taken place after a period of a year or so, depending upon how long it would take for slower money growth to trickle down into the rest of the economy. The actual result was something else.

TABLE 2: INFLATION BETWEEN 1975 AND 1980[12]

YEAR	CONSUMER PRICE INDEX (CPI)
1975	10.8%
1976	7.5
1977	7.9
1978	8.8
1979	9.2
1980	10.2

Instead of heading downhill as money growth shrank, the inflation rate did one quick dip of 3.3 percentage points to 7.5 percent in 1976 and then started climbing again, reaching 10.2 percent by 1980. In 1981, prices rose by an awful 12.5 percent, indicating serious problems with the Bank's policy. In fact, the next year, Bouey threw in the towel on targeting M1.

One problem that the Bank had not counted on was that, at the same time it was trying to level prices off, the OPEC countries decided to jack up crude oil prices for the second time in a decade. As the higher sticker price for that liquid gold increased the costs of other goods and services, consumers were once again faced with soaring prices.

According to monetary theory, the problem should have been correctable by controlling the appropriate money indicator. Unfortunately, during this period, chartered banks and other financial institutions created new monetary instruments that acted like cash but were not picked up in the M1 measure. The alternative types of money meant the Bank was likely targeting the wrong indicator to determine the direction of inflation.

Regardless of the reason, gradualism was not the institution's most shining moment. As the economist Peter Howitt said: "After six years of gradualism, the rate of inflation was even higher than it had been at the outset. The Bank decided that a much stronger dose of monetary restraint was needed, even if it resulted in a recession."[13]

TURNING OFF THE SPIGOT

That was an understatement. If the Bank's gradualist approach in the late '70s was an effort to cushion the effect of tighter money on the Canadian economy, its foot-on-the-garden-hose approach to blocking the money supply in the early 1980s was puritanical economics at its worst. Canadians were about to pay the price for decades of neglecting the rate of price increases and running big budgetary deficits.

Using a broader measure of the money available to Canadians, it is obvious the central bank was turning off the spigot fast and hard.

TABLE 3: GROWTH IN MONEY SUPPLY[14]

	GROWTH IN:		
TIME	M2	M3	CPI
Q1'81	15.2%	14.7%	15.4%
Q1'82	9.9	6.5	13.2
Q1'83	7.6	5.6	5.0

In just two years, the Bank constricted the growth in the national money supply by more than 50 percent, which in turn chopped the inflation rate by almost 70 percent. That's the good news. But here is the bad news. To accomplish this task, the central banker caused the worst recession since the Great Depression of the 1930s.

Between July 1981 and January 1983, Canada endured six straight quarters of negative real GDP growth. Two quarters of minus numbers back-to-back is enough to put the economy in a recession (by the technical definition). This bad economic patch during the early '80s was three times as long.

The outcome of the monetary slowdown was seen in interest rates, which reached 21 percent in 1981. People stopped borrowing, businesses halted expansion plans, and the jobless lines grew. The unemployment rate, which stood at 7.3 percent for the first quarter of 1981, hit 12.5 percent in the same three-month period two years later. In fact, Canada would not see a single-digit unemployment level until 1986, five years later.

Finally, the economy began recovering in 1982 and, by the middle years of the decade, was chugging along nicely, albeit with higher unemployment. Of course, Friedman's theories never promised to solve a country's jobless woes, only its price problems.

For those who were in the Conservative government of Brian Mulroney, this would be an appropriate point at which to finish the story of Canada's monetary gyrations. After all, the Tories had embarked upon a two-staged reform of the income tax system, which eventually included the introduction of the Goods and Services Tax and the negotiation of a politically tricky free trade deal with the United States. The ruling Conservatives had enough economic booby-traps with which to contend. Ottawa did not need more problems from the Bank of Canada.

CROW FINISHES THE JOB

Unfortunately, Mulroney, the boy from Baie Comeau, would have no such luck. John Crow, an acerbic English expatriate who now headed the Bank, ran a raze-and-burn campaign against the country's 4 to 5 percent inflation rate. Crow was a monetarist in outlook, especially in his view that the central bank had very little effect on the unemployment levels, either up or down. In his mind, joblessness was a function of the real side of the economy, not the monetary end. Anything he did would not significantly affect the unemployment levels. Relieved of the responsibility for Canadians without work, Crow wanted the rate of inflation pushed as close to zero as possible. He decided that managing the public's expectations concerning future prices hikes would be far easier if the Bank showed inflation no mercy.

Mulroney's government, with a number of former business types like Michael Wilson, the finance minister, publicly applauded the policy. Under Crow's program, however, the increasingly unpopular Tories faced rising interest rates, questionable economic growth, and a potentially soaring federal deficit. Worse still, the provinces would endure growing fiscal problems because of the coming recession.

Similar to 1981, interest rates began climbing in the late 1980s, reaching 12.8 percent in 1990, up 36 percent compared to the 1988 level of 9.42 percent. Predictably, Canada's economic growth slowed, as national income shrank by 1.8 percent in real terms in 1991, compared to the 2.4 percent positive growth rate of two years earlier. And, again like clockwork, the national jobless figures started creeping northwards. In 1992, approximately 11.3 percent of Canada's workforce sat at home without jobs as compared to a jobless rate of 8.1 percent in 1990.

Finally, Canada tipped into another difficult recession, this time spanning 1991 and 1992. Unemployment was up, growth was down, and consumer confidence was in the tank. But at least inflation had finally been tamed. By the early 1990s, Canada's rate of price increases plunged to less than 2 percent and has stayed in that range ever since.

These days, analysts debate not whether Canada is facing renewed inflation, but whether the country is entering a period of deflation, when the general price level drops for a sustained period of time. At this point, the burning question among that boring lot of analysts who watch the Bank of Canada and run through their Enigma machine each statement made by the governor was whether Canada's crushing of inflation was a victory or a defeat for traditional monetarism.

David Laidler, a University of Western Ontario professor, chief Canadian torch-bearer of the monetarist crown, and possibly the country's sharpest economic thinker, argues that the attack by Bank governor John Crow applied Milton Friedman's money theory at its best. He figures that the most important indicator of an economy's monetary stance is the size of the interest-rate spread between the yields of long-term and short-term fixed-rate financial instruments. Laidler says, Do not zero in on monetary indicators like M1 or the absolute level of interest rates to gauge how tight or soft the grip of the central bank is on the money supply. Instead, economists should keep an eye on how the prevailing interest rate on treasury bills relates to the so-called overnight interest rate: what banks charge securities dealers to borrow cash for a very short period of time.

In Laidler's words: "The T-bill/overnight spread is a key indicator of the extent to which the Bank of Canada's policies are contributing to, or offsetting, disequilibrium between the supply of money and the demand for it."[15]

Using this measure, the Bank of Canada's restriction on the national money supply reached its nadir in late 1990 when the overnight interest rates charged by banks exceeded the treasury bill rate by 75 basis points, or 0.75 of a percent, a huge amount by financial standards. That meant that financial institutions could borrow necessary funds only at a higher premium than prevailing interest rates. As a result, they were more likely to rein in excessive lending as a cost-cutting measure.

The subsequent tightening of the money available in the system led to higher interest rates and a general economic downturn. Inflation was defeated and the sun finally began to shine on the economy. In the view of Laidler and Robson, monetarism led to this brave new low-inflation world: "The re-emergence of a monetarist view of the workings of policy was equally gradual and accompanied the Bank's growing commitment to its policy goal."[16]

THE BANK'S VIEW

The only trouble with this resurrection of the listing theory of monetarism is that the Bank did not agree. In the view of the shadowy bureaucrats who inhabit the Bank's green-glassed towers on Ottawa's Wellington Street, the government's goals were best served by targeting an actual inflation rate rather than any kind of intermediate economic indicator, such as M1. Instead of manipulating monetary levers and hoping for the best, the government should just figure out what inflation rate is acceptable and hike or lower interest rates accordingly.

In February 1991, the Bank announced it would begin targeting inflation specifically, with its first signpost set at 3 percent by the end of 1992. By mid-1994, this guide had been reduced to 2.5 percent, and to 2 percent by the end of 1995.

Initially, the central bank and Ottawa were worried about the one-time inflationary shock that likely would result from the introduction of the new GST. In 1990, Iraq had invaded Kuwait, causing a worldwide jump in oil prices. The Bank and the government wanted to make sure that inflationary fires, which had been so hard to put out ten years ago, would not be reignited by another temporary oil shock.

Hence, just as when Trudeau instituted wage and price controls fifteen years earlier, the country's monetary authorities wanted to send signals to businesses and individuals that the central bank and the federal government were serious about beating the stuffing out of inflation. This they did. Ask anyone taking a passing notice of the economy whether the Bank of Canada or the federal Liberals were committed to keeping inflation down and you got a resounding "yes."

That does not mean that all economic actors are happy with this policy. After all, Canada's unemployment shot up, reaching 11.3 percent in 1993, and has dropped only gradually.

The U.S. has a jobless rate in the 4 percent range, close to the average after the Second World War. On the other hand, Canada still faces an unemployment rate hovering around 8 percent.

Many people blame the Bank's continuing tough monetary stance for the country's poorer job performance.[17] In the two-handed world of economics, other analysts blame the unemployment rate on Canada's generous social programs, laws that interfere with business, and a tax structure that penalizes hard work.

Whichever explanation one accepts as the true cause, and regardless of whether monetarism was the big winner or grovelling loser in the effort to wring inflation out of the economy, the story of money supply as a saviour of the country is at an end.

After all, Canada's obvious economic problem is an unemployment rate that is twice the American average. Rightly or wrongly, the Bank and the federal government have wrestled inflation to the ground with precious little indication of its near-term revival.

THE MONEY THEORY STUMBLES

Monetarism's great failing is that it has nothing to say about creating jobs except that the government cannot help. In a sense, Friedman's money theory has come a cropper on the same problem as Keynes's gem of the 1930s: relevancy.

Keynes wanted to solve unemployment and basically succeeded, but he had no answer for rising prices. Friedman attacked the economy's persistent price woes but was essentially no help on the job front.

Other industrialized nations underwent a similar trial by monetary fire as did Canada. Britain endured huge amounts of labour unrest during the 1970s. By the end of the decade, the U.K. electorate had finally had enough, voting in Margaret Thatcher as prime minister. That country's first female head of government proved herself to be tougher than any previous leader, staring down the militant miners' union and thumping Argentina in the Falklands War.

Thatcher also ushered in Britain's experiment with monetary targets. But her government ran into the same trouble in implementing a monetarist policy as other nations, namely the inability to control the aggregates. As a result, her government reduced the money flow to a dribble and interest rates climbed. Eventually, the U.K. economy slowed and national unemployment rose, prompting a nosedive in Thatcher's popularity as the general election of 1983 approached. Fortuitously for the Tories, the Argentinian generals picked 1982 to try to steal the Falkland Islands back from the British. The Iron Lady won the subsequent shooting war and soared in popularity, achieving a huge victory in the next vote. While her reputation for toughness was intact, Thatcher's strict monetarism lay in tatters.

A quick rethink among her brain trust led to a more microeconomically based industrial strategy. The government's program consisted of reducing the power of Britain's labour unions and abolishing municipal councils (a hotbed for Labour activism), among other difficult to implement policies. As well, Thatcher's Tories pushed the privatization of publicly owned corporations on a wide scale and the deregulation of industry in many areas. By the middle part of the '80s, the British economy picked up. But Thatcher was no longer touting strict monetary controls.

The U.S. administration of Ronald Reagan picked an even stranger route. The Republican government headed by the former movie actor watched as the American central banker, Paul Volcker, cranked up interest rates to deal with soaring inflation. As in other industrialized countries, the U.S. rate of price increases plummeted.

Unfortunately, at the same time, Reagan decided to implement Arthur Laffer's supply-side tax cuts to keep the economy growing. This economic consultant had convinced some prominent conservative thinkers that what was needed to boost the American economy was a large tax cut. That prescription was not new. Laffer brought forward the belief that these reductions be self-financing in a short period of time because of the entrepreneurial burst of activity that would result.

What grew instead was the budget deficit, as borrowing costs increased sharply and quickly dropping inflation shrank the government's revenues. In short order, the U.S. went from being a lender of capital to other nations to a borrower of huge amounts of cash from the world's financial markets. At that time, only a few people, such as the 1984 presidential candidate Walter Mondale, talked about the need to get the government out of the red. Instead, wealthier Americans watched as their stock portfolios rose in value; their poorer brethren watched as their income and job prospects fell significantly.

That was the ostentatious '80s when flash was king and junk bond king Michael Milken had hair. Well, his toupée is gone and so are American excesses, well-chronicled in books such as Tom Wolfe's *Bonfire of the Vanities*. Americans are now preaching the value of the information economy and the need to provide some help to the less fortunate.

It seems words like "monetarism" and "supply-side" now occupy the same dusty page in the dictionary of American economics as William Jennings Bryan's "cross of gold" or Galbraith's "new industrial state." Back where it started, monetarism is now an interesting footnote in the history of the Western economies.

As the '90s began, the great struggle of economic ideologies was at an end. The banner of Keynesianism, so long standard fare among all kinds of governments, was now held high only by a hearty band of zealots, led by the Nobel prize winner James Tobin. Monetary concerns were now front and centre in public policy. But, just as inflation was whipped, monetarism fell on its face, beaten by untrustworthy measurement techniques and an inability to deal with the latest concern for many governments, namely the lack of jobs, as unemployment in Canada and Europe stayed around an unacceptable 10 percent.

Worse still, during the gold-plated 1980s, a little-known economic theory had made it onto the academic agenda, subtly at first and then with great force. Its influence was not felt among public policy advocates, partly because its tenets were initially seen as too bizarre to be useful. But the rational expectations theories of Robert Lucas and his cronies were the neutron bomb of academic economics. And no one would survive its potent rays.

Six

THE STRANGE WORLD
OF RATIONAL
EXPECTATIONS

WHAT HAS ROBERT LUCAS GOT TO
DO WITH ULYSSES GRANT?

It is an irony of history that, often, as the great battle is being joined on one front, a person is toiling or an event is occurring in some less important area that will eventually decide the outcome of the titanic struggle. In 1861, in the United States, the Union general Irvin McDowell and the Confederate commander Pierre Beauregard were waging war in the first battle of Bull Run. Meanwhile, in the forgotten theatre of the Midwest, Ulysses Grant was taking his lumps against some tough Confederate troops. Four years later, Grant would be accepting the surrender of Robert E. Lee at Appomattox, while McDowell and Beauregard had long passed from the scene.

In economics, the 1960s and '70s witnessed a fierce struggle between the incumbent Keynesians, trying to defend their demand-push theory while coping with rising inflation, and the attacking monetarists, who did not believe you could reach economic nirvana by spending money you did not have. Meanwhile, in an obscure economic outpost in Minnesota, a pair of academics at the Federal Reserve Bank of Minneapolis decided to throw their lot with a University of Chicago academic and form one of the most iconoclastic and influential schools of thought in the post-war era. "One day, after reading a paper by the economist Robert Lucas, [Neil] Wallace walked into the office of another Minneapolis Fed research consultant and U of M professor, Thomas Sargent, and announced that everything the two economists had learned until then would have to be thrown out the window."[1]

Although few recognized the immense importance of the group, their theory of rational expectations would eventually shine in the economics field like a bright star on a dark night, obliterating any trace of neighbouring orbs. The era of ultra-rationality was about to hit economic thought, changing forever how people studied the business cycle.

Rao Aiyagari, a researcher at the Minneapolis Fed, said, "It is unthinkable today to analyze questions in macro and monetary economics in the old pre-Lucas way."[2] The theory, which became known as rational expectations, has been described as "the single most significant theoretical development [since the 1970s]."[3] It netted its inventor the 1996 Nobel Prize for economics.

As much as the system of rational expectations has received praise, the theory has also been called "wacky-sounding" and its advocates have been accused of having "just leaped off the pages of Marvel comic strips."[4]

Even more surprising about this new thinking was that its supporters were not proposing any major shift in public policy, as Keynesians and monetarists had done in past decades. Lucas, Wallace, Sargent, and Robert Barro, a Harvard University economist who was another member of the group, were not flogging huge tax cuts. Nor were the rational expectationists hyping government spending as a solution to any country's economic woes. Instead, the new classical economists (as proponents of this theory became known) pushed an idea that, on the surface, did not seem very controversial. Once the implications of their thinking were deciphered by mere mortals, however, Lucas and his gang became leaders of a kind of anarchist charge against mainstream theories, smashing the effectiveness of the old thinking but leaving little in place to which politicians could anchor their ships of state.

SIMPLE IS BEAUTIFUL

In his system, Lucas tried to figure out what would happen if you assumed people to be intelligent enough to look at a newspaper or listen to a radio and then make plans according to the information they had read or heard.

Analysts had always assumed that consumers, businesses, and other actors in the economy would pursue their best interest when they were searching for a job or buying a product. What Lucas did was extend that basic thinking to the way these same people anticipated their economic future and government policy. It may not sound very path-breaking, but it was.

Hence, the term "rational expectations": the predictions of economic actors looking into the coming periods in a logical, or rational, way, based upon an assessment of available information.

Lucas wanted to see how the great theories of the day would hold up if you figured people use all the data they can to formulate what they will do in the next days, months, or years. In this world, "people make economic decisions in a way that tends to take into account all available information bearing significantly on the future consequences of their decisions."[5] In other words, they make their future plans in the same logical way in which they would decide whether to take a new job or how much to pay for a product.

A RAIN SHOWER AS ECONOMIC THEORY

Suppose you go into your house from the fresh air of a beautiful spring day. You putz around, cleaning up, and then decide to go out again. You click on the radio and a weather report says a storm is brewing. Rational expectations simply says that instead of grabbing the light jacket that you wore outside previously, you will take a rain slicker. Available information is telling you that you had better modify your behaviour, in this case by wearing a shell, before you head out the door.

Suppose you don't believe the radio report and leave without your shell. The rain pours down and you get soaked. The next time you go out, the chances are much greater that you will believe the announcer's forecast. All this seems stunningly obvious. When facing similar situations, people do not make the same mistake time and again.

Until Lucas pointed this out, however, most prevailing theories supposed that people would not correctly anticipate future events and, instead, would be guided by past, and in many cases incorrect, economic observations. As a result, governments could fool them into making particular decisions even if they were no better off following these new plans.

In conventional economics textbooks, workers, companies, and consumers follow the iron rule of rational decision-making when figuring out whether to pursue a wage hike, price increase, or clothing purchase: they usually try to maximize how much they will benefit from whatever they do. In the case of public policy, however, these same overpriced academic tomes assume people would not pay attention, say, if the government announced a program to bring the inflation rate down significantly, for instance, from 15 percent to 5 percent in one year. Instead, in the prevailing wisdom, they would look at last year's inflation rate, 15 percent, and assume that number, or something close to it, would be the rate in the next period as well.

This logical flaw particularly affects Keynesian thinking. The system figured that governments could affect the overall economy by pursuing different policies depending upon whether demand needed to be increased or decreased.

Using a business cycle example, suppose Ottawa wants to boost economic activity to stave off a recession. The central bank prints stacks of new money, which will drive down interest rates and entice companies to borrow and consumers to spend more. Workers will see their money wages increase and feel good about their future prospects. What they will not see is a looming burst of inflation from the high rate of monetary expansion. The net results would be more demand for private sector goods and services and more jobs for the unemployed.

Eventually, the growth in the national money supply should translate into higher inflation. That means what the unemployed believe is an increase in the salary associated with the new jobs is, in fact, merely a nominal jump in the wage rate. Once the rising price level is taken into account, the jobless person is now working for the same pay packet he or she refused to accept before the government started printing more money.

But, for Keynesian demand stimulus to work, people need to make this miscalculation over and over again.

Lucas had a different view. People would be unlikely to keep making the same mistake repeatedly. They would learn from past experience and recognize the future consequences of current public policy.

And, because of their improved ability to predict the future, people would frustrate the government's ability to stimulate the economy, whether through spending decreases or interest rate decreases.

THE OLD GUARD ON DEFENCE

The rationality assumption was not really an ingredient in Keynesian or even in monetarist thought.

Suppose Ottawa wants to boost its spending to reduce national unemployment. Remember Chrétien's "crane in the sky" infrastructure program in 1993. The government orders a few new frigates, builds a highway or two, and raises a couple of hockey arenas in some desolate part of the prairies. The new money flows into these areas and companies start hiring new workers. That part of the theory figures that more companies want more people and the unemployment rate falls.

Better still, firms start giving larger salaries to attract many kinds of workers, usually skilled ones. Their incomes go up, another positive outcome of government spending. Here's what Ottawa did not anticipate. Companies now need to hike prices to pay for the suddenly more expensive labour. After all, the salaries of workers who make these products are now higher.

So, firms either boost prices to get additional cash or do not produce as much as previously planned to keep their wage bill low. If they pick the former course of action, prices go up and the average working stiff now realizes he is not better off in real terms, that is, after subtracting inflation, than before the government started spending the extra money. As Carl Walsh observed, "Eventually, workers would recognize that the general level of prices had risen and that their real wages had not actually increased, leading to adjustments that would return the economy to its natural rate of unemployment."[6]

If, on the other hand, firms pick the strategy of cutting back on production, they will not hire the extra workers the government anticipated when it began throwing around the extra dollars.

THE NAIRU DETOUR

To a large extent, this critique of Keynes was developed by Friedman and led him to promote the theory of the Non-Accelerating Inflation Rate of Unemployment as a counterattack against the prevailing tax-and-spend wisdom. As noted previously, Friedman's idea is commonly known by the acronym NAIRU, which sounds a bit like an Australian rabbit but in fact is one of the more powerful concepts in modern economics.

Friedman, a classical liberal, maintained that if an economy faced a particular level of unemployment at a particular moment, that must mean people are unwilling to work at the going wage rate, which may be at a high or low level in nominal terms. According to this argument, if they wanted to find a job, they could knock down the salary they expected to earn.

The question is not whether there are enough jobs to go around but whether people are willing to lower their pay demands to get those positions that are available.

Thus, Friedman believes all unemployment is voluntary in that these people could work if they were willing to chop their starting salary to what an employer wanted to pay.

It is important to realize that he was not concerned about the particular salary level associated with available job openings. The pay rate may be high or low compared to other employment opportunities. That is irrelevant to Friedman. All he is saying is that a person could find work if he or she reduced wage demands.

He also believed every economy has a particular unemployment level that cannot be reduced simply by increasing government spending or cutting interest rates. There was no free lunch in the curmudgeonly Friedman's thinking.

Suppose Canada has an unemployment rate of 8 percent, which cannot be reduced at the current wage rate, and the average salary is $10 an hour. The NAIRU theory assumes the jobless do not wish to work at the going wage rate. Thus their wage demands are too high given the existing level of productivity in the economy.

Now, you have a group of workers who do not wish to work for $10 an hour. Assume that Ottawa's new deficit-financed spending drives consumer demand and eventually wages up to $11 an hour. That increase should entice some of the unemployed to enter the workforce, looking for fatter pay slips. Once firms increase their prices to reflect the higher salaries, however, those workers would be no better off in real terms than before. In Friedman's mind, the employee, finally recognizing his true situation, would quit the job and head back to the television couch.

In this theory, governments can spend as much as the capital markets can stand to lend. It will not matter to the unemployed since the concurrent appearance of higher prices will squeeze them out of the workforce in short order anyway. The only way the government could affect the jobless rate over a longer period would be to continually fool people into believing that they are better off than in reality. In this case, they would enter the workforce even though the wage rate they would receive in real terms had not changed.

To surprise workers and companies, the administration would have to change interest rates without warning or start spending more at the drop of a hat. Without such an unexpected element, economic actors would see their true circumstances pretty quickly. The government's actions would lose their effect. Then the only remaining effect of the public largesse would be higher prices, a bitter harvest from the optimistic seeds of Keynes's theory.

Worse still, people form their expectations of the future based upon the recent past, according to Friedman. Thus, once they figure out a 10 percent boost in the money supply, to stimulate spending, works out to be a similar increase in the existing price level, the only way they can be fooled is if the government accelerates monetary growth even more. The result is that, to keep the same artificially low level of unemployment, the country must be willing to endure higher and higher rates of inflation.

NAIRU DODGES ONE POTHOLE . . .

While academically interesting, the NAIRU concept has problems. The thought process by which these people quit their jobs and go back on the dole, a key facet of monetarist thinking, is never spelled out. Writer Linda McQuaig pronounces absurd the belief that workers, having finally secured a job, will then quit merely because they have not benefited to the extent they initially thought. Why, she asks, would someone quit a job merely because he or she has figured out the effects of inflation on the wage packet? As McQuaig puts it: "Can Friedman really say with any certainty how the average worker will behave when confronted with the fact that inflation has caught up with his or her wages? Is Friedman some kind of expert in human psychology?"[7]

The answer is, of course, he cannot and is not. The implications of McQuaig's critique are that, as common sense dictates, people can be without work even if they do not wish this condition. Perhaps demand in the economy is simply too low. Maybe the search costs connected with looking for a decent job are too high at the prevailing wage rate.

Whatever the reason, Canadians can be out of work through no fault of their own.

In fact, part of this built-in joblessness is due to what economists call "frictional" unemployment. In some cases, people are counted as being without work even though they have only just left one position and likely will have little problem finding another.

In other instances, employers demand a different set of skills than those of the unemployed. For example, Canada continually finds itself short of technology workers even though the country's high level of unemployment suggests there is slack capacity in the national labour market.

This kind of thinking places you right back in Keynes's parlour and his demand management theory. Increasing the amount of goods and services craved by the unwashed masses becomes an option. Or maybe the government could examine ways of reducing the cost of looking for work. This is the thinking behind the policy of allowing people to deduct some moving charges from their income tax. Either way, government has a big, not minor, role to play in the solution.

Perhaps, however, McQuaig's criticism has things backwards. Instead of explaining why they would quit, she needs to tell us why they would stay on the job.

Let's go back to our example. Before Ottawa started stimulating the economy, these workers were unwilling to accept the prevailing wage rate in exchange for work. Why would they suddenly accept that same amount of cash to work merely because politicians are spending more money? If you were unwilling to settle for $10 a hour before, why are you now happy with a nominal rate of $11 and a 10 percent inflation rate? In practical terms, the person is accepting the same amount of money with a job as he or she rejected before securing employment.

If people are logical, at least concerning their own situations, you have to answer that nothing has changed and, therefore, they would be unwilling to work at that wage. The mechanism of how they quit is less important.

As clever as McQuaig's criticism is, she relies upon unemployed people making two errors: firstly, when they enter the workforce by not realizing that the government's policy will ultimately mean higher prices, and secondly, by remaining employed even though they know they are no better off than before.

It is simply a long stretch in logic to believe that the jobless will make these mistakes over and over again, that they will never learn from experience. If one accepts that logical decision-makers learn from their errors, the Lucas-Friedman idea starts making more sense.

. . . . BUT HITS ANOTHER

A more telling critique of the NAIRU concerns the difficulty in measuring the natural jobless rate. Time and again, economists have tried to figure out where the natural rate of unemployment is in such countries as Canada and the U.S. And they have failed.

In Canada's case, estimates for the employment floor have ranged from 4 percent to 12 percent, a three-fold difference, hardly a useful policy-making guide for Ottawa. South of the border, the U.S. has already crashed through the 6 percent unemployment level, which was believed to approximate the NAIRU for that economy, without reviving inflation. Paul Martin has repeatedly said the NAIRU is theoretically interesting but of no practical use. And he may be right. After all, if you cannot measure the NAIRU, then governments still can intervene effectively in the economy as long as they are not approaching this jobless level.

Still, Friedman's attack on Keynes was effective. Rational expectations took the thinking one step further. Remember the ineffective spending example. If employees have already been burned once by government-induced inflation, they are likely to recognize the next time that the only outcome of more public spending will be higher prices. So, far from switching off the television to head for the local employment exchange, these louts will stifle a yawn at the reports of new expenditures and reach for the channel changer because they know they would not be better off by taking a job.[8]

Under rational expectations, a government does not even get the satisfaction of seeing the job numbers rise until workers realize their true situations, at which point employment falls back to its previous point. In the new classical theory, people adjust their thinking right away, negating any positive effect from the additional public expenditures. If they adjust immediately, the government will not get any positive kick from spending more money. Thus, no matter how much the authorities try to stimulate the economy, they are always destined to face roughly the same amount of unemployment.

There are only two ways to lower joblessness. You can squeeze higher productivity out of existing employees, thus increasing profits, a prerequisite for new hiring. Or you can reduce the amount of money one can earn without working, through social assistance or unemployment insurance, thereby giving people the growling stomach incentive to get a job.

MONETARISM UNDER ATTACK

If the policy of incurring deficits to boost the economy does not fare too well under rational expectations, neither does using monetary tools to accomplish the same purpose.

In this case, Ottawa could cut interest rates by injecting more money into the economy. More money in circulation usually leads banks to drop their borrowing charges as a way of getting rid of the extra cash. Once loan charges fall, firms generally start spending on new projects, which ultimately would mean more hiring of those pesky jobless people. Now, the economy has greater levels of capital investment, more production, and more smiling, employed workers.

Splash yourself in the face with some cold water, according to the new classical crowd. Allowing the central bank to put its foot on the monetary accelerator eventually results in higher inflation. Remember the last chapter. More paper floating around the economy *now* tends to mean rising prices in the *future*.

Since economic actors understand what is going on, they would recognize that any money lent now by financial institutions, say, to buy corporate bond issues, will be worth less in the future because the higher price level will degrade the currency's value. In that case, groups would have very little incentive to lend cash without getting juicier returns immediately in the form of, you guessed it, higher interest rates. The government-induced 2 percent interest rate cut then becomes a 2 percent jump in what lenders will ask to accommodate the anticipated increase in inflation.

Once again, the government tried to stimulate the economy, this time by lowering interest charges, a policy commonly advocated for Canada these days, and all it received for its trouble was a higher dose of inflation.

The same academic spear has harpooned both of the great theories of the middle decades of the twentieth century. In the words of one observer, "Imagine how this theory shocks Keynesians and monetarists. Their advice appears as useless as the comedienne Gracie Allen's offer to solve the California-Florida border dispute."[9]

Rational expectations supporters argued that the theory could predict past events reasonably well, an odd kind of history at which economists excel. Clarence Nelson of the Federal Reserve Bank of Minneapolis said that applying this thinking to data between 1965 and 1977 shows "three major upward swings that, loosely speaking, trace a kind of Phillips curve expansionary relationship."[10]

By returning to past years and applying a rational expectations model, economists were able to trace a relationship close to what actually happened. Since making future projections is a difficult way to test a theory, economists often look backwards to check their ideas.

This model might even explain Brazil's recent economic troubles. The Latin American government decided to abandon its policy of maintaining its currency within established trading bands to keep its value stable. Unfortunately, Brazil's currency had become overvalued in the eyes of the world's capital markets, forcing the administration to allow it to float freely. That move immediately caused the currency to drop against the American dollar. But officials hoped the lower exchange rate would also prevent a capital flight. This prediction did not come true, as investors continued to pull their money out of the country. Rational expectations might say that people correctly anticipated that the cheaper currency would lead to higher inflation. Because of their past, many South and Central American nations have a singular lack of credibility when it comes to maintaining a tough line on rising prices. So people are merely forecasting a burst of inflation, which would decrease the value of their investments. Hence, the continuation of the capital flight would be the proper response by investors.

Once the rational expectations thinking made it into mainstream academia, the effect was electrifying. Professors left the halls of political power where they advised governments and headed back to their university offices to grapple with ways of saving their pet theories. All of a sudden, past thinking seemed outdated. Everything everyone had done until now had to be kneaded and massaged in light of rational expectations to ascertain the new results. That intellectual exercise would take time and energy.

Economists had a hard time reorienting their thinking quickly, partly because rational expectations, for all its verbal simplicity, involves formidable analytical tools. New students in the post-graduate classroom wanted to learn rational expectations theory in all its mathematical glory. Whether or not it was comprehensible to the outside world was secondary. Public policy applications now took a back seat to the ascendancy of theoretical economics at universities and think-tanks.

Lest one think that Lucas and his contemporaries have solved all problems economic, however, it is time to see how some academics mounted stinging criticism of the new theory.

RATIONAL EXPECTATIONS ABSORBS A BODY BLOW . . .

The obvious criticism of rational expectations is that people are just not very logical. They make decisions on the spur of the moment, with bad information or in a poorly considered way. So how can Lucas and his cronies assume people will understand the implications of, say, an interest rate cut, and make the correct decision in their economic interests?

As well, there is the question of whom to believe when figuring out what economic evidence to follow. Lucas and his followers assume that consumers and businesses only need to watch one government to get a true picture of the administration's economic policy. In a federal state like Canada, however, different levels of government can change the trajectory of economic policy in a region or even nationally.

For instance, Ottawa controls interest rates, the provinces have a hand in taxation, and the municipalities decide a large portion of the property tax. Figuring out which statements from which authority will be the key ones in deciding one's economic future may be tough, especially if the policies at one level of government contradict the aims of a program implemented by another level.

. . . BUT STAYS OFF THE CANVAS

Before the theory gets dismissed too quickly, however, consider first that many economic groups already use large amounts of information to make decisions. This is especially true in the financial services sector. Whether one is a securities trader or an investor, these people often are information hoovers, sucking up as much data and commentary as possible before deciding upon a particular path.

Or take a union, like the Canadian Auto Workers, entering into wage negotiations. It would be naive to assume this experienced group of bargainers would not use as much forward-looking information and advice as possible about inflation and future economic conditions before sitting down to talk with Ford or General Motors.

Far from being irrational or silly, many key groups already approach their coming economic decisions by studying mountains of available studies and information.

Secondly, and perhaps most importantly, Lucas and the others are not saying people make the proper choice each time they decide upon a course of action, but that people will not keep making the same error repeatedly. Rational expectations figures most groups learn something from their mistakes and will alter their behaviour the next time they face the same situation.

OTHER PROBLEMS

The new classical theory says that markets must clear, or get to a final point where supply meets demand, very quickly. Rational expectations supporters have argued that, in most situations, this free market point exists and can be reached in short order.

Let's go back to financial markets. When something happens on the stock market, the news is almost immediately reflected in the price of the equity, altering the supply and demand. The price of the stock gyrates right away depending upon whether the news is good or bad for that particular firm.

For many economists, however, the notion that all markets find their proper equilibrium, the place where someone is willing to sell and where someone is willing to buy a product or service swiftly, is a large pill to swallow. That would mean wages go up and down equally quickly and that product prices fall and rise in fast order, both ideas that Keynes rejected.

In short, the theory does not allow for market imperfections or barriers. Monopolies exist; workers sign long-term agreements; a small number of firms essentially fix selling prices in some industries. There are a number of impediments preventing people from reaching the market-clearing equilibrium quickly, or at all.

In other cases, the very rationality of various participants in the economy can work to ensure that the proper outcome is not reached. Here's an example. It is often true that, when an economy's output jumps or falls, the country does not immediately return to the old level in the next year. Say Canada's GDP rises by 10 percent because of an unexpected burst of overseas demand for our goods. Even if those extra buyers disappear in the next twelve months, the national economic output will not immediately fall by the same amount. That decrease will occur over time.[11]

Now add in rational expectations. If you assume that people are forward-looking, you have to believe that they know the sticky tendency in national output and will incorporate it into their thinking. So in the beginning, a government stimulates the economy and gets a higher level of output in return. People will recognize that now the economy will remain at this new GDP level for some time and consumers will adjust their demands accordingly. In effect, the government would boost the economy just like under Keynesianism.

Finally, some of the predictions flowing from rational expectations theory just do not appear to have come true. For instance, following Lucas's logic, countries should be able to reduce the level of price increases without enduring gut-wrenching recessions. Assuming you have a government that is credible when it announces an anti-inflationary policy, workers and businesses would recognize that the national authority was serious about smashing prices and, in response, would fall into line. People would start dropping their wage demands and firms would begin cutting what they charge.

That does not appear to happen in real life. The Liberal government may not have been credible when it began pursuing lower prices in 1981. But people did eventually believe Crow in the late 1980s when he said the Bank would try to stabilize prices. Yet the 1991 recession was as nasty as the one in the early part of the previous decade. And the jobless levels are only now beginning to decrease substantially. As Professor Roger Ashton McCain explains, "Rational expectations tells you what would happen in a perfect economic world. Unfortunately, we don't have a perfect economic world."[12]

In the midst of all this teeth-gnashing by the academic community, any useful policy implications for rational expectations were lost. The only really practical bit of advice that these theorists have given is the need to announce targets for a government's anti-inflation policy ahead of time. Then people, being rational animals, will take the figure into account when they make their plans.

Even here, how people find out about the Bank's commitment to low inflation can be a mystery. After all, most Canadians do not spend their days perusing the *Globe and Mail* or watching CBC Newsworld, waiting for the latest public statements from the Bank of Canada.

Regardless of its utility, this bit of rational expectations advice has been followed to a tee in Canada. The Bank of Canada now states targets in advance for the rate of inflation, putting all groups in the economy on notice. At least the years of hiking interest rates and the resulting brutal economic downturns have filled Canadians with the confidence that, when the Bank talks tough about stopping inflation, it is serious.

ECONOMICS AS NIHILISM

Regardless of its intellectual merits, expectations theory has not been very useful for policy-makers. Inflation was tamed by the effective but hardly subtle program of jacking up borrowing costs to stop companies dead in their expansionist tracks and by ratcheting up the level of unemployment to scare workers into accepting small wage gains, or even unchanged pay.

To help the jobless, Lucas's theory really only says that there is not much that can be done. Look to other economic policies, like training or cutting the minimum wage, for your solutions.

So politicians faced a difficult choice. They could stand up to the electorate and say, You'll just have to face long-term high levels of unemployment. That was the idea of Kim Campbell, the Tory who was prime minister in the early '90s barely long enough to let her coffee cool. She said Canadians would have to accept double-digit unemployment for many years, no matter what government was in power. Not only was she wrong in fact, she misjudged people's capacity to accept continuous bad news. Voters had tired of leaders who told them what was impossible, and they clobbered her by returning only two Conservatives in the election of 1993.

Or a government could jettison any pretence of following an economic theory and instead implement policies that are popular. This is the pragmatic, anti-intellectual theory that governments have subscribed to in the past decade. Harris's tax cut, an election plank endorsed by precious few economists, is an example. Voters saw in the reduction an administration willing to do something for the average Ontarian.

Never mind that any stimulative effect of the cut would partly be negated by federal payroll levy increases and local government tax and user fee hikes, mainly due to the province's cutting its funding to pay for its tax cut. Never mind that the loss of revenue meant that Canada's largest province would also be one of the last to balance its budget. Even the basket-case, normally fiscally profligate PQ government in Quebec beat Harris in eliminating the deficit. Here, in Ontario, was a new kind of administration, one willing to help the silent majority of taxpayers and to pursue policies the other parties were scared to try.

This is the short-term legacy of Robert Lucas. In economic theory, the Chicago professor is the last great revolutionary of the century. He threw intellectual bombs that destroyed the walls of academic complacency and forced a bunch of smug economists to go back to first principles to rework their thinking. In the eyes of some observers, the fresh thinking has resulted in new analysis and new revealed truths in economics. "The young stars [in academia] of the 1980s had a well defined and compelling research agenda — the application of rational expectations to the policy world — which is now more or less complete."[13]

Perhaps. But if the complete agenda contained much in the way of macroeconomic policy recommendations upon which governments could act, especially to reduce unemployment, no one is letting on. Lucas had smashed any basis for an activist policy by government. Nothing any administration could likely do would have much effect on the economy, in his world. So the message is, don't try.

Yet problems remain. Productivity is a pressing concern, although measurement differences make it difficult to grasp how serious it really is. Yet all the think-tanks can do is talk about tax cuts, a policy bound to harm our ability to pay down outstanding debt and one with little evidence supporting its positive effects on productiveness.

Worse still, to pay for these cuts, the government must reduce spending, likely in the area of social programs. But are not these institutions, the schools, hospitals, and the like, important parts of the productivity equation in the first place?

And round and round the arguments go, in favour of spending or tax cuts or debt reduction or something else. All of the debates, however, founder because they have little intellectual backup. Instead, Canada is left at ground zero in terms of economic policy. As at the impact point of a nuclear bomb, nothing grows in this barren intellectual environment any more.

Most governments in many countries have abdicated using consistent, modern economic theory to map out a program to reduce unemployment further and set the country on a better footing in terms of national income growth.

As Thomas Sargent puts it, "There's a schism between research being done on the frontiers of macroeconomics and thought in policy circles. Most economic policy-makers in Washington show little acquaintance with macroeconomic theory in general. It's very hard to tell if their thinking is guided by any kind of model."[14]

In a way, Lucas and Friedman are the same. Though able to shatter any residual confidence in big government, neither Friedman's monetarism nor Lucas's rational expectations could offer anything to take Keynes's place. Both are good at hammering existing ideas but lousy at presenting policies to achieve the same goals.

These two economists' notions of small government and free markets do not stem so much from the logic of their theories as from their personal beliefs. (In contrast, Tom Sargent, one of the most prominent new classical thinkers, also is known in academic circles as a Democrat and a liberal.)

Friedman and Lucas were able to articulate the damage done by governments pursuing economic policies. But they were only to replace the present platform with a straitjacket that called upon people to give up most of the benefits and protections they already enjoyed in order to throw themselves on the not-so-tender mercies of the marketplace.

Their economic system is not based upon policy benefits but upon a quasi-religious teaching that says people must sacrifice to reach a greater good. Low-income workers should accept a lifetime with no guaranteed minimum wage secure in the knowledge that they are helping the market to operate more efficiently. Fishermen, miners, and other seasonal labourers should be happy with lower unemployment benefits, recognizing that they are being forced to train for another job or move to another region for their own good. Welfare recipients should embrace cuts to their benefits because less cash in their pockets will get them into the workforce faster.

Basically, conservative economists want people to swallow a lot on faith. Accept a decrease in your living standard now and you might be better off later on . . . although we cannot actually guarantee any actual improvement.

Newspaper editorial writers often decry the population's short-sightedness for not embracing market-based notions with open arms. In fact, these thinkers are the woolly-headed ones. Those media types, the popular purveyors of radical conservative theories, are essentially religious zealots who decry others' beliefs while theirs are sitting upon the same kinds of shifting philosophical sands and questionable logic. Groups who disagree are labelled cranks. Often, their own plans are based upon breathtaking leaps in logic and lack even the most minimal evidence.

Canadians are unwilling to sacrifice everything that has raised their lifestyles over the past number of years on the strange calculation that accepting actual decreases now will allow them to reach some better economic plateau in the future. No wonder they are embracing conservative economic thinking less enthusiastically than its proponents had hoped. Of course, voters have bought into *some* tenets of the theory. After all, conservative administrations were elected in many countries during the 1980s. And even Liberal governments have, as a practical matter, appropriated part of this platform to stay in power. The miscalculation these commentators and backroom activists made was in overestimating the desire of Canadians to follow a back-to-basics approach to public policy. Conservatives believed people were ready for governments to get out of their economic lives and into their social ones.

You can see the logical connection. If Canadians wanted less government regulation in the marketplace and lower deficits, maybe they would be keen on tax cuts, a return to tough standards in the classroom, and — who knows — anti-buggery laws. That is where the country's neoconservative experiment came to a screeching halt.

IT'S THE DEFICIT, STUPID

Canadian economic conservatism was, and remains, really about two things: the economy in general and the elimination of the deficit in particular.

Starting in the mid-1970s, analysts in this country became increasingly alarmed as governments piled up more and more debt by way of yearly deficits. Using the analogy of the average household balancing its books, bank economists and other equally adventurous types convinced Canadians that something had to be done to reduce this growing tide of red ink. After all, the national credit rating and, ultimately, those social programs that many people cherish, were at risk from the public borrowing.

As well, Canadians needed a new yardstick by which to measure the performance of governments. The public sector had become such a huge and complex beast that many voters had long since given up any hope of understanding its behaviour. Instead, they looked to some simple measurements to tell whether Ottawa or their provincial administrations were operating relatively decently.

In past years, the unemployment and inflation rates served this purpose. If either variable rose too fast, voters would hold politicians accountable in the next vote. In the 1990s, however, the electorate needed another gauge with which to understand Ottawa's performance. This time around, inflation was useless since it had been tamed and, with the loss of faith in Keynes, unemployment appeared an intractable problem, reducing its value as an indicator of the government's quality. It became hard to tell whether, with a persistent unemployment rate of at least 8 percent, the government of the day was doing a good job or a bad one.

During the last decade, people focused upon the deficit as the new yardstick for public performance. Reducing governmental red ink became the way an electorate assessed the performance of Ottawa and the provinces. In these tough political times, "small deficit good, big deficit bad" was now sober thought among the electorate.

To some degree, the success of conservatives at getting the deficit agenda into the brains of public officials killed their chances at pursuing a wider program of market-based reform and social change. As soon as governments started balancing their budgets, people began looking for the money to be returned in the form of new spending or tax cuts.

Neither alternative was really based upon an economic theory but rather on simple politics. When faced with such uncertainty, politicians usually pursued the policy most likely to secure their re-election. And that is what happened. Liberals promoted their ability to balance the books and Tories talked about giving those in need a helping hand and everyone, except Mike Harris, gingerly tiptoed in the direction of tax cuts.

It is important to remember that, during the late 1980s and into the 1990s, economics continued to advance even in the face of the Lucas Revolution. In fact, Keynes had made a comeback in universities in a new form, one that explains economies in terms of imperfect markets by using such real world phenomena as labour contracts to emphasize the lack of fluidness in many sectors.

Unfortunately, much of the new debate stayed in classrooms and learned journals, an interesting discussion reserved for the PhD seminars or technical conferences, not for grubby political backrooms. Instead, the discourse in this arena had taken a distinctly pragmatic hue. Party platforms contained policies often internally inconsistent, but designed to appeal to the largest number of voters.

For instance, the Ontario Conservatives' tax platform was designed to appeal to upper and middle class voters who felt under siege by governments looking to expand their revenues. Economic consistency was not the issue, winning an election was.

A similar sort of policy anarchy reigned throughout many governments in Canada, the United States, and Europe. Administrations had chucked any pretence of discovering a useful and consistent set of economic principles upon which to base their government. Instead, backroom wheeling and dealing became the order of the day.

THE MEDIA YACKHEAD AS SAVIOUR AND VILLAIN

In public forums, academic economics have conceded the ground to a group of "policy entrepreneurs" — as Paul Krugman labels them — analysts, usually residing in think-tanks or financial institutions, who promote particular policies in a simplistic fashion to maximize their public profiles. One example is Laffer and his supply-side theory, in which an idea sketched out on the back of an envelope became the rationale for the largest deficits in American history.

In Canada, too, a number of these quasi-academics have burst onto the public scene, dominating the debate in the media, often at the cost of real discussion.

Most recently, Sherry Cooper, Paul Volcker's former right hand, now chief economist at Nesbitt Burns Inc., launched a verbal assault on the nation's airwaves, calling for large tax cuts as the only hope for dealing with a falling Canadian dollar, failing productivity, and just about any other economic problem one could think of. Jeff Rubin, another Bay Street talking head, joined the chorus in favour of chopping federal rates to boost the currency, a policy that previously he had maintained would hike consumer spending.

Krugman, an effective public figure in his own right, accuses these kinds of economists of stumping for their own personal agendas, not arguing with academic precision. To some degree, he is correct. These cardboard thinkers are essentially politicians: they are flogging a position or policy and will scramble for any available evidence to support their case. They are not interested in the latest debate except to the extent they can use it to muster a case for their pet idea, in this case large tax cuts.

In a sense, however, Krugman is engaged in a rhetorical exercise of his own, in which he shoots all the inmates of a jail to make sure he gets the few guilty ones. In fact, policy entrepreneurs serve a real purpose in the public discourse surrounding economics. Whether it is Galbraith, MIT professor Lester Thurow, or some other offender of Krugman's rule requiring pristine academic debate, these people serve as the communicators of theory to politicians and the general public. They are the ones who translate the current, often impenetrable, thinking into a core of ideas that elected officials and opposition members can use to develop a debate on the economy.

Krugman evidently thinks government bureaucrats and elected members ought to spend their time thumbing through academic journals and attending university conferences in the hope of discovering the latest public policy developments in the attributes of econometric models or the most interesting mathematical ways to prove a particular theorem.

In Canada, at any rate, political staffers, bureaucrats, and ministers do not get their information in this measured way. Instead, they quickly flip through *The Economist* or glance at CBC Newsworld or some equally enlightening television channel, all in the hope of catching some idea that can be translated into a political platform.

Hence, think-tank and brokerage house academics serve an important purpose for politicians. Without them, parties would be left to fend for themselves when it comes to devising ways to boost the economy.

That's the state in which Lucas has inadvertently left the Canadian political scene. The only people willing to venture forth with ideas have been the same old group of economists, too interested in promoting the interests of their clients, usually by pushing some combination of government spending reductions and income tax or payroll tax cuts.

That left this country in the weird position of just now fighting debates like whether tax reductions will lead to a huge explosion in government revenues, discussions that are not part of the public discourse south of the border.

FINALLY SOME HELP

Fortunately, as the 1990s advanced, a couple of thinkers came to the fore, two men whose ideas were advanced a decade ago but are now current in the country's political and business hallways.

The first of these to pop his head above the surface of the debate over inflation and business cycles was the economist Paul Romer. While more prominent members of his profession debated expectations and the likely results of government activism, Romer began pushing the frontiers in the obscure area of economic growth theory.

The other, Robert Reich, a Harvard lawyer and public policy thinker, began synthesizing different lines of thought into a new industrial organization theory about how corporations work.

Reich pushed the idea that how large companies divided the work among their various divisions determined the economic structure of a country. As a result, governments should worry about attracting the best parts of these huge corporations to their jurisdictions, not about whether the firms will be profitable in their areas. Let management take care of their earnings. Administrations should figure out how to get the best workforce possible to attract the leading edge parts of global corporations.

These theories can be welded together to form a new policy structure to push Canada and other countries into the information age. Fundamentally, debating whether a particular tax cut or spending increase will boost growth or productivity is sterile. What countries need to know in the future is how to make their workforce as efficient and effective as possible and how to give companies the tools to compete at a time when innovation and discovery, not the level of capital formation, is the key to growth.

The industrialized countries of North America and Europe are poised on the edge of the new information age, where capital and labour are no longer close substitutes, where firms set up operations in different countries, and where an educated, healthy, fully employed workforce is no longer a goal but a necessity. In this era, the theories of Reich and Romer provide the keys to Canada's ability to ride the new wave of technology to a growing and prosperous future.

SEVEN
GROWING
INTO PROSPERITY

At first glance Paul Romer seems an odd choice as the great saviour of interventionist governments. This forty-three-year-old self-styled former libertarian is the son of a former Democratic governor of Colorado, Buddy Romer. He bristles at the idea that his thinking could be used as a justification for big government.[1]

With his mop of unruly hair and oversized glasses, Romer looks more like an aging keyboard player for an '80s electronic group like The Cars or Level 42 than a prominent economic theorist. And he has made his name in a relatively forgotten area of economics, one that has not been probed much since the 1960s: growth theory.

Yet, by toiling in this out-of-the-way zone of academia, Romer has crystallized one of the big problems facing the dismal science and has given governments new ways of addressing an old issue. Better still, once you meld the so-called endogenous growth idea of Romer with Robert Reich's description of today's corporations and labour market, you get a reasonable way to attack Canada's persistent unemployment problem.

It is important to recognize that no theory is likely to solve the country's jobless woes entirely and bring the unemployment level down to 2 percent or so. By adopting new policies in line with these theories, however, Ottawa can give Canada's workforce the confidence that its competitive advantage will be centred on skills and education, and will not evaporate at the first sign of an economic downturn. Government must ensure that employees are not forced to decide between wage cuts and the loss of jobs to unskilled Third World labour.

Romer and Reich, working as they do south of the border, may not realize it, but their theories give Ottawa a logical approach to unemployment and growth that will move Canada's economy into the twenty-first century.

REVIVING KEYNES

While hanging the millstone of greatness around the necks of Romer and Reich, we should acknowledge that other thinkers have also been hard at work moving economic theory beyond where Lucas left things in the 1980s.

In fact, in the past decade or so, a substantial body of literature has sprung up from academics interested in resurrecting liberal values and, gulp, dear old J. M. Keynes. Gregory Mankiw, George Akerlof, and others have developed effective replies to the rational expectations attack on older policies.

These new Keynesians rely upon models of the world in which imperfect competition prevails to give a pretty good case for activist government. They use the common sense view that, in fact, markets do not immediately, if ever, clear, or reach a point where demand equals supply.

Firms have access to different amounts of information at different times, making their reactions variable, and they have incentives to keep prices high even during a recession. The new Keynesians play to the strength of J.M.'s theory. Rather than aiming for academic perfection, it appears to better fit the real world than most other schools of thought. In the words of Mankiw, "If Keynesian economics was dead in 1980, then today it has been reincarnated."[2]

Indeed, while Lucas and his crowd were prominent in the last decade, they do not have too much to say these days. In fact, Lucas has partially abandoned business cycle macroeconomics to join his former pupil Paul Romer and thrash around in the less travelled waters of growth theory.[3]

Even if the new liberals have begun to recapture the ivory towers, they have had little impact upon policy-makers, especially in Canada. New Keynesians may carry some cachet in the lecture halls and on the pages of obscure economic journals. For most politicians, however, they have all the relevancy of Egyptologists rummaging about in ancient tombs. The new Keynesians are not to be found among the advisers of current governments. Chrétien and Paul Martin do not have them in their Rolodexes. And their voices are not often heard in the major media.

THE POLITICS OF SHOUTING: CONSERVATIVES IN THE '90s

Conservative economics may have hit a brick wall in logical terms. The effectiveness of its supporters at presenting their case in the media, however, means this thinking still dominates the mindset of many voters and elected officials.

Neoconservative forces march on, even though the movement relies upon spent intellectual forces, like the Fraser Institute in Vancouver. Journalists seem to be unable to find more interesting commentators than the same crowd of pontificators who have made wrong predictions and peddled faulty logic for the past ten years.

Some Canadian commentators talk about tax cuts as if Reagan's supply-side experiment had never taken place. Friedman's views are still revered by these analysts although he has not been particularly relevant since the 1980s. And, as far as Robert Lucas is concerned, governments, editorial pages, and think-tanks do not appear to have caught up with the theoretical advances he pioneered twenty-five years ago. To them, Lucas is the guy who created *Star Wars*.

One of the latest machinations of these public policy brain surgeons was the hysterical call in late 1998 for quick and large tax cuts as a way to restore the value of the Canadian dollar and the country's competitiveness. Some Bay Street brokerage houses, whose clients would likely be the biggest beneficiaries from such income tax reductions, stumped for that view with abandon on talk shows and in newspapers.

To be fair, their plan has some logic. They argue such a cut would boost Canada's productivity by enticing a burst of entrepreneurial energy from the country's downtrodden wealthy and middle classes that toil under the current onerous regime. Our income tax rates are high, at least in the upper income levels, compared to those of the United States. But critics neglect to mention the productivity-enhancing benefits these tax dollars have bought, such as a first-class health care system.

Besides, a prediction of some sort of Prometheus unbound effect from rate reductions begins to sound suspiciously like Art Laffer's over-optimistic supply-side predictions of the late '70s.

As well, Ottawa's budget could fall back into the red because of a sharp tax reduction. That likely would send currency traders into a tizzy and the dollar into a downward spin, the very thing the cuts were supposed to prevent.

In fact, Canada's currency problem stabilized when the new European money became a partial reality last year and traders began to recognize that Canada had relatively strong economic fundamentals. Indeed, the dollar has gained some strength this year, and some sober-minded economists, like Warren Jestin of the Bank of Nova Scotia, think the loonie could crack 70 cents (US) by the year 2000.

The appeal of Canada's neoconservatives to the chattering classes is difficult to explain. The country's editorial pages and policy institutes remain in the grip of Tory blue or Reform green. In these public forums, the only people yapping about solutions are the same lot of righties such as William Watson, and lefties such as Mel Watkins.

Sadly, except for an occasional flash of brilliance from seldom-heard-from economists like the University of Western Ontario's David Laidler, you could be forgiven for believing the big economic debates of the past fifteen years had not occurred in Canada at all. Indeed, one would have to comb the newspaper pretty closely to find any discussion about rational expectations or new Keynesianism. And only the *Toronto Star*'s David Crane has talked about Romer's ideas. Most other columnists spend their time declaring Keynes dead and trying to breathe life into the increasingly rancid corpse of supply-side economics.

One explanation for Canada's backwardness in public policy is that political and economic trends just seem to hit here five to ten years later than in other parts of the industrialized world. Conservative thinking, which infected Britain and the United States in the mid- to late '70s, had to wait another half-decade before Brian Mulroney began to advance mild market-based policies, like selective tax reductions and a North American free trade agreement. His government, however, never approached the free market zealousness of either the Americans or the British.

Finally, Canada has its first two U.S.-style conservative premiers in Klein and Harris. At the same time, however, House of Representatives Speaker Newt Gingrich has dropped from the American political scene and his "Contract With America" is not mentioned any more. Indeed, you see provinces introducing balanced budget laws, taxpayer referendums, and all sorts of government-inhibiting rules just as administrations in other countries are wondering whether these restrictions actually serve any purpose.

Maybe it is timidity on the part of our politicians or an innate Canadian caution that allows other countries to take the lead on public policy before we decide to follow suit. In any case, economic and political trends generally hit these lovely shores a few years after everyone else has accepted or rejected them. So, while Blair's England and Clinton's America show the first signs of toying with a new interventionist agenda, Canada is not pursuing much of anything. We're like a country on a life raft in the middle of the ocean. The boat has to get to land, but which direction to take remains an open question.

ENTER PAUL ROMER

Early in his career, Romer, a Stanford University economics professor, decided that wading into the great debate over inflation was a waste of time. Friedman and his counterparts had done a good job harpooning Keynes's system.

But Friedman et al. could not really offer much of a replacement. The monetarists had little to say to people about how to get jobs, ensure their children would be better off, and guarantee national prosperity. At these points, the monetarists' closet is pretty bare.

You need a job? In a perfect theory, all unemployment is voluntary. So cutting your wage demands should do the trick. Governments can help by eliminating minimum wage laws that prevent workers from reducing their salary hopes.

Try growth. If the government cannot get you a job, maybe the economy will create one of its own. That is the kind of anti-government thinking Friedman and his crowd applaud.

Unfortunately, their theory does not offer much else. Growth is a function of a country's productivity. These economists might say that reducing lavish social programs and eliminating union power are good ways of boosting the economy.

The best monetarism can offer is a rule for maintaining the growth of the money supply at a constant rate. Then, theoretically at least, the natural competitive juices in the rest of the economy will be able to flow.

This is not a very satisfying vision for politicians seeking power or for people grappling with a falling standard of living. Friedman, however, never promised anyone that prosperity was easy to achieve, only that, much as in medieval Catholicism, you would get your reward somewhere else for a generation of patience, chastity, and frugality.

In some cases, Friedman's extreme application of market-based prescriptions left people scratching their heads. For instance, he has argued that the U.S. Food and Drug Administration, the government agency that tests drugs and the like, should be eliminated. The axing of this bureaucracy would speed up the time in which healing substances make it to the market and lower the level of suffering in the country.[4] Try telling that to mothers who took untested substances during their pregnancies only to give birth to deformed babies.

These free market suggestions may be interesting academic exercises. Most reasonable people, however, are left wondering on what planet these professors reside. Debates such as these have all the relevance of one graduate school seminar at Carleton University in the early 1980s in which the doctoral candidate outlined the mathematics for his economic theory of marriage. Again, perhaps interesting, but to what end?

Besides, voters are unlikely to accept a full-blown retreat by governments from their obligations to improve the overall quality of life. That is because people are not entirely economic animals and have other concerns, prejudices, and interests than pure income maximization.

They might recoil at the questionable logic of inflicting untested drugs on an unsuspecting population. Not surprisingly, no major political party has adopted the full range of policies advocated by monetarists and other free market types, lest they appear hard-hearted or out of touch with voters.

Romer approaches economics from a different, and fundamentally better, angle. The intellectual food fight between liberals, monetarists, and rational expectations specialists essentially concerns how best to smooth out the peaks and valleys of the business cycle. They are focused on solving a short-term problem: a year-long recession or a six-month inflationary spike. Once the present situation, be it high prices or poor job prospects, is addressed, then the economy can get back on track, the so-called non-inflationary growth path.

WHAT ABOUT GROWTH?

In this debate, Romer asked an obvious, but largely ignored, question: Would it not be more fruitful to figure out how to raise the trajectory of the long-term economy, rather than fight over how to deal with short-term blips?

On one level, this question implies some simple logic. You must make sure the foundations of your house are solid before you worry about what colour to paint the trim. Or, a country must have the proper policies in place to ensure that its economy will grow at the maximum rate over a number of years before worrying about the prospects within a single twelve-month span.

As with everything in economics, however, the first answer is not always correct. Many market-based analysts argue that their policies are already aimed at the long-term goal of raising the country's overall growth rate. Once the government has wrung inflation out of the system, for example, then businesses and consumers can get on with the task of building a stronger economy based upon welfare maximization.

As pointed out earlier, however, their theories revolve around lifting the economy's inflationary veil and allowing economic actors to recognize the true financial situation and act accordingly. But that notion only gets the country to the beginning of the growth path; it says nothing about the road itself. It's as if these economists quit after stuffing the daredevil into the cannon, forgetting about the gun's trajectory and whether a net is properly set up to catch the poor soul.

Keynes had a different approach to getting the economy on its long-term growth path: Essentially forget it, or at least, don't worry about it to the exclusion of other considerations.

Many analysts believe the struggle for long-term policies is a chimera, a worthy but unattainable goal. The reason is that unforeseen problems are always preventing an economy from reaching its steady state nirvana.

In the past, oil price shocks, political referendums, the unforeseen collapse of Asian economies, and other events forced governments to respond quickly to economic situations by changing their plans. Also, the electoral cycle is usually too short for administrations to engage in fundamental long-term planning.

Making policies to get their economies on some textbook-like trajectory seems ludicrous in the context of everyday political and financial contingencies. You are better off getting a handle on the business cycle than plugging away at an idea that makes sense in an introductory economics class but that needs too much time to work or is politically unrealistic.

Still, finding a way onto the proper long-term path is important, at least to focus a country's intellectual energy. Asking people to sacrifice income or their peace of mind for an economic goal in which the benefits may be only indirect only works if they believe they are contributing to a permanent improvement in the nation's financial state and their own living standards.

Telling people to give up possible salary hikes to deal only with an immediate oil price increase begs the question, What will you ask from me when the next crisis comes? Governments are on far firmer ground arguing that concessions are important for the economy's longer-term health than for a short-term problem.

Besides, the global economy is changing as information technology becomes more ubiquitous and the older manufacturing industries decline in importance. In that context, figuring out the proper paddle to use — which monetary and fiscal stance to maintain in the face of a recession or an overheated economy — is important. Finding a new waterway through the continent, however, remains the overriding goal.

And Romer is a modern-day Lewis and Clark, looking for a better way to negotiate the great unknown, in this case, economic expansion. Instead of a canoe, his weapon is growth theory. Figure out the sources of growth, he argues, and you have discovered the economic equivalent of the fountain of youth.

No one would argue with that goal. Conservatives and liberals alike want economic growth, either to pay for tax reductions or for further expansion of social programs. The debate is about how to get the growth you desire.

REWORKING THE THEORY

Until the 1980s, growth theory essentially started and finished with Robert Solow, the 1987 Nobel Prize winner for economics, and his neo-classical growth function developed in the '50s. Other thinkers, such as Walt Rostow, attacked this area, but without Solow's formalism.

His simple equation[5] mixed together the proper levels of capital and labour to get robust economic growth. When you worked out the mathematics of Solow's formula, population growth became a crucial factor underlying the economy's growth. Innovation was important but was viewed as God's gift to an economy — not a factor over which elected officials have much control.

That left capital accumulation as the one big factor driving up national income over which governments have some effect. According to Solow, if a country attracts new foreign money or entices its population to boost their savings, better economic growth will result.

A flaw in this system, according to Solow's argument, is that a country expands indefinitely by continuously adding capital in the form of new machines. Find a way to attract foreign investment or get your own people to save more cash, and you will always improve your economy.

That kind of thinking, however, runs afoul of a basic economic principle — the law of diminishing returns. As a nation adds more and more capital, eventually the new investment will not be enough to increase the stock of machines, once depreciation, or the rate at which existing machines deteriorate, is included. As one theorist said, "Higher rates of investment do not lead to increases in the net capital stock or output."[6]

Now, a country can no longer simply keep adding machines and money and grow at the same, or faster, rate. As economists put it, capital exhibits decreasing returns to scale, which means that as you add more and more of something, beyond a certain point the benefits you receive in return get smaller and smaller.

Think of a textile plant. You have ten workers and no machines. You add the first loom, and you get a large increase in productivity because you are now making some garments whereas before you produced nothing. Add another machine, and you double your output since you now have two workers in action, one on each loom. Everything works fine until you get to the eleventh machine. Once that begins operation, you now have to have at least one employee using two machines. You will still get an increase in output, just not as large an increase as if you still had one worker per loom. Add a twelfth machine and the extra output is less again because now two employees are splitting their efforts.

The law of diminishing marginal returns is paramount in economics. It allows newer firms a chance to catch up to more mature enterprises that may have already reached the point at which the returns from new additions are falling.

Once you account for diminishing returns, Solow's theory spins off one interesting implication, namely that the income levels of countries should converge, or approach the same level over time. As they add more capital, economic laggards will enjoy a burst of growth just as the leading nations are reaching the limits to what new machines can add to their national income.

What you should see then is that less-developed countries grow faster than more mature, industrialized nations, allowing their GDPs to creep closer together. The result should be all nations improving their standards of living with poorer ones growing faster than richer ones.

Wait a minute, what about technology? Aren't improvements to production processes and the discovery of new ways of doing things the real driving force behind economic progress? It might be nice that you can add a larger number of horses to the herd. But you could still only get to point B as fast as the old grey mare was willing to travel. It was the creation of the automobile, a new technology, that led to shorter travel times.

Of course this observation is correct. And Solow recognized it. But he had no satisfactory way of modelling improvements of this kind and stuck with his characterization of innovation as an afterthought from God, at least figuratively. And it was asking a lot of even the brightest economist to devise ways a government or firm could get the Supreme Being to fork over a greater number of innovations. As with many of the stickiest problems in the dismal science, this variable was ignored or assumed away.

As well, Solow's depiction of economic growth did not fare well in its predictions. The less industrialized and industrialized worlds did not converge as he expected. Plot the growth rates of countries between 1960 and 1985 and it is readily apparent that poorer countries grew no faster than richer ones.[7] Remember, under Solow's set-up, most poorer nations should have enjoyed growth rates that would allow them to get closer to the industrialized economies. Instead, in many cases the disparity between rich and poor has widened.

INCREASING RETURNS TO SCALE

Romer believed he had a way to explain these counter-intuitive results. He argued that innovation was not "exogenous," or from outside the system. Instead, technical progress was something created within the economy, or "endogenously." That is important because if innovation comes from a country itself, then governments and companies can assist in the discovery process.

Administrations can institute policies that give people an incentive to find new or better ways to do something. Maybe Romer cannot predict which innovation will happen. If a government follows the proper program, however, the country will enjoy a faster rate of technological progress than other nations. That is different from previous thinking.

Better still, according to Romer, new discoveries exhibit increasing, not decreasing, returns to scale. Here, he focused on the so-called "spillover" effects which have led to this best of all worlds. People who make a first discovery tend to share with others the new information in some form, if not the actual physical process. The second group is able to make use of the principles discovered in one situation to make a second innovation. So, from one new way of doing something comes a batch of new solutions to other problems. Thus, the economy grows at an accelerating rate.[8]

Unlike the decreasing returns to scale assumption, the increasing returns principle means the economy benefits by the same amount, or more, from each additional discovery. In essence, there is a very high ceiling on how much a country can benefit from more innovations.

Accordingly, in Romer's world, nations that invest heavily in people or machines, the raw material of innovations, should enjoy faster and faster rates of growth. These improvements to existing production processes, or to the way discoveries build upon each other, speed up growth. Frankel states, "Economies with higher saving rates [to invest in machines] will grow faster, and so convergence [of national growth rates] in the neoclassical sense need not obtain."[9]

Of course, like any other economic theory, Romer's growth ideas have come under fire professionally. Some critics argue that, if innovation is the key to expansion, the United States should lead the pack every year because the Americans are the most innovative country, as measured by the number of patents filed annually.

Still, Romer's theory makes government policy important as a way of boosting the country's rate of technical innovation. Armed with this insight, Romer can offer a better explanation as to why poor countries still lag behind richer ones. The more industrialized nations could innovate faster and hence maintain their growth advantage over less developed countries. The increasing returns to scale of these innovations accumulated in advanced countries, pushing their growth to higher peaks.

Not only does Romer's theory paint a picture more closely resembling reality, but government now gets a role in the new economy, establishing ways to boost the country's innovation rate. He suggests, for example, extending the scope of patent protection laws and letting the private sector direct research and development in post-secondary institutions.

But Romer's theory does not necessarily lend itself to a larger, more interventionist role for government. Remember he is very leery of the ability of governments to devise the proper policies to rev up the technology engines.

ADAPTING THE THEORY TO CANADA

In this country, however, Romer's theory takes a decidedly different turn. Establishing a program based upon such subtleties as allowing the private sector the lead role in directing innovation might make sense in the United States with its 250 million people, marvellously efficient economy, and broad base of large multinational enterprises. Canada, however, needs a more direct approach. Canada has only 30 million people and an industrial structure composed mainly of subsidiaries of foreign corporations. Canada's economy is too small and regionalized to expect the optimum level of innovation to grow naturally from the private sector.

As well, foreign-owned companies are very likely to keep the research and development function at their head offices south of the border. In that case, the spillover effects, which are crucial for Romer's theory, are less pervasive up here. This problem has existed in Canada for a hundred years.

What is new for this country is Romer's increasing returns to scale hypothesis. If he is correct, that means the one who is first out of the blocks likely will be the one to win the race. As an economy begins making new discoveries, the rate at which these innovations are uncovered speeds up. The lagging economy can develop new processes on its own but is unlikely to reach the level or the rate of growth of the first country.

In the normal economic world, a company has a difficult time maintaining an advantage as it grows. That is because the smaller, more flexible firms can achieve expansion rates that outstrip the first business. Decreasing returns to scale hamper the leading firm's ability to grow and its large size hurts its ability to react.

In a world of increasing returns to scale, however, the first firm that starts on the innovation track likely will win the game, piling up a larger lead over the rest of the field. The initial improvements that the company uncovers will lead to more and more innovations and a faster rate of growth. Other companies also have to make new discoveries that will improve their business prospects to remain competitive. These firms, however, probably will never be able to overcome the initial advantage of the market leader.

This is not the scenario in which giant IBM in the 1980s suffers from an inability to read the new computer market. It is the one in which Microsoft takes over the world. The software company made some key innovations, gained a business lead, and was able to exploit the new technology to find other discoveries, increasing its commercial head start even further, until it became dominant.

Look at Romer's increasing returns to scale problem in a different way. Japan and Germany achieved a remarkable economic recovery after being bombed into oblivion in the Second World War. In these two cases, the countries borrowed technology and innovations from other countries, especially the United States, and added their own touches. The result was that these two defeated enemies became powerhouses, surpassing victors like England in economic progress. Neither country had to be a market leader. Instead, they could be economic followers and use that situation to make fewer errors and take advantage of their superior rates of return on capital to boost growth.

That will not be true in a world where innovation, which exhibits increasing returns to scale, is the key to economic growth. In that case, neither a Japan nor a Germany would ever be able to make up for their technologically backward state in the beginning. Their living standards would improve but never enough to approach the other industrialized nations.

If Romer's theory is correct, why didn't economies exhibit increasing returns from innovation after the war? How could defeated countries, like Japan and Germany, catch up to the victors in living standards?

This is where the information highway enters the equation. That vast array of computers, Internet ports, cellular phones masquerading as data devices, and other bits of hardware and software has changed everything. These systems exhibit the increasing returns to scale in their networks in the same way that the innovative process does.

Think of the information highway as the physical embodiment of innovation. You have pieces of glass, bits of metals, and lines of code on a disk, nothing too daunting to replicate. However, the capacity of computers, the Internet, and the like to absorb and manipulate information is very high. It does not cost a company additional money to place more information on its network. The cash is all up front to pay for the initial system. The only effective limits become the ability of the human brain to absorb such a large amount of information so quickly.

Once again, the first out of the gate in the race for information supremacy is the likely winner. That is because the second player has to invest a similar amount of cash to get his network up and running. Then he has to overtake his competitor who already has a commercial lead and is running faster because of his initial and subsequent innovations.

Suppose you're the first company to establish a nation-wide communications system that links Internet users in a useful way. You have already built the system; all you need to do is add customers, something that does not cost extra cash for new capital, only some money for marketing and those functions. So, the price to new customers is pretty low.

Better yet, you don't really have to save cash to add more capacity for these extra people since the width of your data pipeline is already virtually limitless. You can push new customers on your system without paying to improve the network's size. Meanwhile, your competitors have yet to fork over the dough needed to build an information network of their own. They fall further and further behind. This race may already be over before it has started.

The last couple of years in the world's information industries show that this scenario, admittedly stylized from Romer's innovation theory, may already be upon us. North American and European phone carriers are gobbling each other up at an alarming pace. Canada's telephone companies have had to quickly link up with U.S. giants — witness Bell Canada's alignment with the U.S. phone heavyweight Ameritech — or risk extinction.

Computer makers are examining ways to compete with communications firms. The rate at which these changes are taking place is dizzying. Why? Well, perhaps the fight is over capacity, and the one with the biggest pipes at the starting line wins. These firms may recognize that, if they can be one of the top two or three suppliers of information technology, they will survive and have a sufficiently large data network to allow them to add customers and fight the few remaining firms on an equal footing

Maybe the economy could rely upon those new, fast little guys, the usual source of competition in North America.

Not likely. These tiny companies, as they develop, will look to jump onto one of the existing platforms, not try to create their own. After all, these existing players already have a size advantage that is enhanced by the increasing returns that information technology exhibits.

What makes this situation more distressing is the importance of information technology to future economic growth. Everyone from Clinton to Gilder to Manley has cited the crucial function that communications and data movement will play in the new economy. Manufacturing and resource extraction, while not dead by any means, are becoming less important pieces of the modern industrial economy.

Technically, the new king of the industrial heap is the service sector. Even in the United States, 70 percent of all economic activity is based upon the selling of services, not the trading of goods. Within that figure, however, the most important portion is not the country's ability to give better haircuts, but the nation's facility with the sending and receiving of data. Phone carriers and financial institutions are examples of industries that will live and die in the coming decades according to their ability to move and manipulate bits and bytes.

If Romer is correct, it is crucial that Canada get out of the blocks in the race for informational supremacy. Lagging behind the field in data transmission only means we will fall further behind over time. And, since these information fields constitute the most important piece of the service pie, slipping on the way to the information highway would doom us to status as a backward nation.

NICE THINKING, BUT SO WHAT?

Canada needs to improve its ability to innovate. According to the OECD's innovation index, this country slipped to ninth place by 1995, down three spots from nine years ago.[10] The study measures the number of patents filed, the level of national research and development spending, and similar indicators.

The role of government in our small economy is important to developing colleges and universities in the area of research and development. As well, Ottawa has to make sure that the private sector is involved so that such innovation is commercially applicable, not just a neat bit of logic for the academic journals.

The information highway, however, is only one part of the equation. After all, for decades, the country has built the economy on the backs of the hewers of wood and drawers of water. These days, companies do not base their competitive advantage on the cheapest labour. Anyone can set up a manufacturing facility in Vietnam or Indonesia. But firms have an increasing capability to divide their corporate functions among a number of countries. The trick for industrialized countries, such as Canada, is to get those pieces of a company to locate here.

Governments could try to use the carrot of lower tax rates to attract new industry. That factor, however, is not that important compared to labour productivity and other factors. Besides, your tax advantage is only a winner until another country decides to drop its rates lower.

Part of the answer is first-class infrastructure, like the information highway and the Internet. But another big piece is training and education policy. And that leads us to Robert Reich, Clinton's former secretary of labour. He has been described as a visionary and as a charlatan. He also is the most understandable embodiment of the kind of education and training policy that Canada must apply if the country is to be competitive in the twenty-first century.

EIGHT

A DIMINUTIVE GALBRAITH
FOR THE 1990s

"People fortunate enough to have had an excellent education followed by on-the-job experience doing complex things can become steadily more valuable over time, making it difficult for others ever to catch up. In fact, their increasing advantage may extend beyond a single generation, as their extra earnings are invested in their children's education and training. Such widening divergences may be endemic to a global economy premised on high-value skills rather than on routine labour or capital."[1]

"The need for governments to double and redouble their efforts to sharpen young minds has become a matter of survival."[2]

It is a cliché these days to say that we are living in a global, knowledge-based, information-intensive economy. Using these terms to describe the economic environment, especially in advanced industrialized countries, has been in vogue for a decade or more. Though these words are losing their meaning the more they are used, they do describe a reality that many Canadians implicitly understand. Change is the imperative. Technology is the means. And uncertainty is the norm.

The question for governments, therefore, is what constructive role they can, or should, play in preparing and retooling a society to ensure prosperity in this new economy everybody is talking about. In Canada's case, even though the country is closer to the ideal of a knowledge-based economy today than a decade ago, we remain more reliant than many of our major competitors on our resources and traditional "smokestack" industries. Minerals and natural wealth used to be the core advantage of national economies. However, unlike Canada, many countries simply lack comparative advantage in these sectors and, therefore, have no choice but to gravitate to knowledge-based sectors or service industries. Yet the nature of Canada's economic structure, along with the fact that the country is trade-oriented (the highest level of trade in the G-7 nations), makes it more vulnerable than its competitors to the forces of globalization. This was driven home in 1998 with the sharp decline in the value of the Canadian currency due in large part to the weakness in international commodity prices.

Hence, in Canada, there is clearly a role and responsibility for governments to encourage and help the necessary transition to a knowledge economy. Leaving this task to the free market alone, as neo-conservatives would have us do, risks relying upon our current, but gradually eroding, strengths and advantages in the old economy and lagging behind our major competitors in the move to the new environment. Coming generations would pay for this lack of foresight and action through the coin of a weaker and less competitive economy and a stagnant labour force.

ROBERT REICH TO THE RESCUE

Half a century ago, John Kenneth Galbraith, a six-foot-six-inch tall economist born in Elgin County, Ontario, arrived at Harvard University, via Berkeley and Princeton, to teach economics. He would go on to hold important positions in the U.S. government and become a key adviser to the long-forgotten Democratic presidential candidate Adlai Stevenson and to President John F. Kennedy.[3] Galbraith remains a timeless symbol and famous proponent of activist government, through both his voluminous writings and his public service career. He was one of the first professional economists who had the ear of an American president, in part because he was a brilliant writer and gifted speaker — traits uncommon in his profession — who tried to communicate complex economic ideas to politicians and the educated masses. University of Toronto president Robert Pritchard described Galbraith in a 1997 lecture as the most famous living economist.[4] He was correct.

Galbraith became influential because he could break serious and complex problems down into digestible bits that elected officials and the common Joe could understand. He could then outline some solution that made intuitive sense. These rare gifts made him a target of younger economists more interested in mathematical eloquence than in communicating with the outside world and influencing policy. As a result of his approach, Galbraith has been denigrated and ridiculed by the economics profession, even though he was actually once president of the American Economics Association, the most important group in the profession in the United States.

In the early 1980s, another distinguished academic, Robert B. Reich, nearly two feet shorter than Galbraith, arrived at Harvard University's Kennedy School of Government, where Galbraith, one of his mentors, still nominally worked. Like Galbraith, Reich receives little respect from economists despite his many influential writings on economic policy.

Reich's educational credentials consist of a master's degree from Oxford, where he studied as a Rhodes Scholar, and a law degree from Yale. Still, without the requisite doctoral degree, he has never been granted the glittering prize of tenure and the academic respectability that goes along with it. Unfortunately, both Galbraith and Reich are victims of economists' revenge: the rejection of those who leave the confines of the academy and attain positions of influence or decision-making authority in the outside world, where they can put often esoteric ideas into action. Krugen's "policy entrepreneur" put-down illustrates the condescension, envy, and scorn that some university economists pour on those who manage to get the public's ear and influence government decisions.[5] (It is an interesting irony that Krugman and his ilk revere the entrepreneur, and themselves grapple with questions of policy, while having nothing but disdain for the policy entrepreneur.) Maybe the fact that many academic economists suffer from this high-minded perceptual dysfunction goes to show that Keynes truly is the greatest economist of the twentieth century. He alone is revered in the profession and also influenced public policy profoundly.

After Bill Clinton appointed Reich to be his secretary of labor in 1993, Reich tried to implement some of the ideas he had developed in his popular and influential book *The Work of Nations*.[6] In this readable volume Reich did not develop path-breaking theory, as Paul Romer did with his often impenetrable contributions to the new growth theory debate. Reich, however, made some important, and ultimately influential, observations and arguments on the nature of the emerging global economy and the appropriate role for government in this new order. His ideas are particularly applicable to Canada, although he wrote primarily with the U.S. economy in mind.

Reich argued people had to think more deeply about globalization, rather than simply trying to increase trade in goods and services.

Beginning in the 1980s, he saw a new global economic system emerging that was rendering obsolete economic nationalism and policies that grew out of what Reich called "vestigial thinking." This was an important observation with serious implications, if true, because administrations throughout the industrialized world had been spending a great deal of taxpayers' money over the previous decades designing policies to push domestic industry, protect culture, and generally get in the way of free markets. European governments had invested billions in "national champions" in different sectors such as automobiles and aerospace. The Americans overtly discriminated in favour of their own aerospace and defence industries, mainly through military procurement decisions, and Canada subsidized sectors such as aerospace and natural resource industries and put in place elaborate foreign ownership restrictions in broadcasting, banking, telecommunications, and cultural industries.

According to Reich, such policies are misguided in the new global economy and betray a misunderstanding of the nature of the coming public policy environment. Large corporations that dominate the emerging economy cannot, in his view, be labelled American, British, French, or Canadian companies in the traditional sense. Instead, they are highly decentralized entities, with offices, subsidiaries, joint ventures, sub-contractors, and networks spread throughout the world, combining components and labour from many countries to produce a finished product or service. A Ford car, at one time a basic symbol of American know-how, can no longer really be called American because it is now designed, manufactured, and assembled throughout the world. More importantly, a vast global web of knowledge workers now exists so that what is traded between countries is "less often finished products than specified problem-solving, problem-identifying and brokerage services," all of which are combined to create value,[7] and value added is the coin of the realm in this economy.

In Reich's view, the most successful firms are shifting from high volume to high-value-added business. No longer is stamping out plastic widgets faster than the other guy enough to carry the day. Instead, products now embody sophisticated design and manufacturing processes. In this world of global, high-value enterprise, the key assets of a firm are not tangible things "but the skills involved in linking solutions to particular needs."[8] The factory worker and resource extractor, whose high wages and ever-growing incomes made the Canadian economy sing in the 1950s and 1960s, are giving way to the knowledge worker, or "symbolic analyst," in Reich's terminology. Symbolic analysts are a new class of highly literate, numerically sophisticated, well-motivated employees whose economic value is based upon their abilities to manipulate analytic tools, such as words, numbers, and graphs, and thereby simplify and make sense of complex problems and masses of information. In short, this crowd is adept at analysis, whether it is of financial data, design questions, legal arguments, or public policy conundrums.

In Reich's opinion, workers in this new class are quickly becoming, if they are not already, the most important asset of firms and advanced economies. In this environment, the only true competitive advantage "lies in skill in solving, identifying, and brokering new problems," which means it is now "the jobs people do rather than the success of abstract entities like corporations, industries, or national economies that determine their standard of living."[9]

To buttress his case, Reich points out that a steadily diminishing share of every dollar spent in an advanced economy is going to traditional production workers, whereas symbolic analysts, or knowledge workers, are commanding ever-higher salaries and fees. One obvious and admittedly extreme example of this phenomenon is the increasing number of management consultants who earn six-figure incomes, call themselves professionals, and convince firms that their pricey services are required for them to succeed. They did not exist twenty years ago.

The shift in the advanced economies from blue-collar workers to white-collar knowledge employees is also reflected in declining unionization rates and a corresponding diminution of labour's political power. Reich summed up these global economic dynamics neatly when he wrote, "The standard of living of a nation's people increasingly depends on what they contribute to the world economy — on the value of their skills and insights."[10]

Reich may have pushed his case too hard when he argued that there is no such thing as a national firm any more. As well, his theories about high-value industries and international competitiveness are regarded as utterly fallacious by some economists.[11] But Reich's point about the importance of skills and knowledge in an economy where firms increasingly use the fruits of technological innovation and compete globally are bang on: indeed most mainstream economists do not argue the point any more. Of course, Reich was not the first to make the case for human capital development.[12] Nor did he necessarily make it better than others. However, *The Work of Nations* was one of the first attempts to popularize these ideas, which resulted in their becoming influential in public policy debates in the United States and elsewhere. For this reason, Reich deserves credit, something economists are loath to concede to him because, in their view, his thinking is not original and is rather woolly. He is one of Krugman's "policy entrepreneurs" who do not understand the basic economic theory that underlies their analysis and policy prescriptions. But holding Reich to an academic standard when he is addressing a popular audience misses the point. Many of Reich's ideas make common sense and have worked their way into government thinking, unlike those of the vast majority of university economists.

If nothing else, Reich was articulating a consensus before there was one. Today, the critical and increasing importance of human capital development seems so obvious and uncontroversial; indeed, a mere eight years after the publication of *The Work of Nations*, Reich's arguments about boosting education and skills training are mainstream and self-evident, although, not surprisingly, neoconservatives still haven't embraced them so far as to support any sort of public investment in these areas. After all, carving out a role for government is antithetical to their free-market, state-curbing ideology. Knowledge and skills have always been important to a firm's or nation's competitiveness, neocons will argue. So there is nothing new or interesting here.

What is different now, however, is that in the old days you could get by nicely with a relatively small, elite group of knowledge workers at the pinnacle of the private enterprise hierarchy, with a mass of less educated, less skilled or knowledgeable drudges supporting the pyramid. But, to be successful in today's global knowledge industries, it is increasingly important to have the whole economic structure filled with well-educated and highly skilled people.

Average wages for people with only high school educations have dropped dramatically throughout the industrialized world since the early 1970s. The income gap between rich and poor, which has widened over the past two decades, has afflicted Canada and the United States in particular and is directly related to education and skill levels. These days, without at least one university degree or college diploma, your chances of reaching the upper income level are negligible. Analyses of Canada's labour market have unanimously concluded that employment and earnings of individuals with only high school education have declined substantially, while job prospects for those who have post-secondary educations have risen sharply in the past twenty years.[13] The Economic Council of Canada concluded, in one of its last studies before being unceremoniously axed by the Mulroney government, that workers with little education and training had steadily lost ground over the previous twenty years in earning power, job security, and ability to get new work. Those with strong educations and training, by contrast, were doing better than ever.[14]

The Chrétien government, in its 1999 budget, reached a similar conclusion, and pointed out that, since 1976, the number of jobs for skilled people, measured by educational attainment, has increased to 5.3 million from 3 million. On the other hand, jobs for the unskilled have remained essentially stagnant over the same period, increasing to only 3 million from 2.4 million.[15] Such data led the government to conclude that "the strong rate of employment growth over the past few years has been highly concentrated in knowledge and information-intensive sectors of the economy that require highly skilled workers" and, for this reason, "developing a highly skilled workforce is . . . crucial."[16]

To make the point even more strongly, three labour economists from Dalhousie University concluded that, in 1990, people with a university education earned 38 percent more than high school graduates.[17] And that was before the big shifts in the global economy towards knowledge-intensive work. While the jobs and earnings benefits associated with higher education are somewhat greater in the U.S. than in Canada, the trend is in the same upward direction.[18]

Reich, Thurow, and other thinkers were thus correct to point out early on that knowledge is now truly at the cutting edge of competitiveness and that human capital development is key to our economic future. But this should not be feared, nor should we lament for the old economy, as some Luddites would have us do. In a sense this new economy is empowering people as never before; there is nothing more self-fulfilling than the attainment of knowledge, education, and skills. Firms are now realizing that their best assets walk out the door at the end of each day, and that recognition can be nothing but good news for employees. An economy structured on this basis amounts to a higher level of development for a country and should be enthusiastically embraced. In this milieu, there are fewer and fewer reasons for not educating yourself or for thinking that you can prosper without good schooling and advanced skills. People should no longer be under any illusions about tying their futures and those of their children to industries that do not require such attributes.

The days of the father watching proudly as his son follows him into the plant or mine are over in Canada. The old economy industries that required high school or less will not succeed in the future, and in many cases could fail to survive in today's economic environment. One illustration of this fact of life is Ottawa's recent and painful decision to end decades of subsidies to inefficient and unproductive coal mines in Cape Breton, effectively signalling the death of this industry and throwing 1,700 miners out of work. Worse still, most of these men have no other marketable skills because they operated under the heroic but anachronistic assumption that the government would subsidize the mines forever.

In the old days people used to say get a job rather than pursue more education, or "less learning and more earning." Today, however, the slogan should be what former ghetto-dwelling NBA players tell kids, "Stay in school."

At first blush, the economic environment described sounds very Darwinian and survival-of-the-fittest. And in one sense it is. The ubiquitous tariff and non-tariff barriers that once gave domestic firms significant cost advantages over their international rivals, and allowed them to be less efficient and innovative, have been disappearing rapidly for a decade or more through international trade agreements like the North American Free Trade Agreement, the European Union, and the General Agreement on Tariffs and Trade. Despite rising protectionism in some countries, notably the United States, it is hard to believe that anyone could significantly unwind the trade liberalization of the past two decades. Even the Chrétien Liberals, once fierce opponents of Canada's trade deals, could not bring themselves to honour the now forgotten 1993 Red Book commitment to renegotiate certain parts of NAFTA. Nor would we want to turn our backs on trade liberalization; freer trade is a laudable and sensible economic objective for any society.

Fortunately, Canadians, for the most part, are not asking their government to return to the protectionist days of the past. They do, however, want their elected officials to prepare people for the new competitive environment that results from freer trade and increased use of technology. Canadians seem to recognize that government has a critical role and responsibility to help get individuals the education, skills, and knowledge they will need to survive and thrive in this new economy.

Boil Reich's theory down, and observe trends visible to anyone willing to take a look, and you find no surprises. Education will be one of the key determinants of Canada's economic performance in the twenty-first century. Reich's advocacy of a new infrastructure agenda based on education is not unlike that of Galbraith's relentless calls during the '50s and '60s for heavy government investment in traditional bricks and mortar infrastructure, which was critical to economic performance during that era. In this sense, Reich is truly a Galbraith for this decade in that he argues for a stronger role for government in improving and building the systems or infrastructures that will be required for an advanced society to prosper in the future.

REICH WORKS BETTER IN CANADA

The United States does not have the strongest tradition of government financing for post-secondary education. So Reich's arguments are a harder sell there than in Canada, which may also help explain why he comes in for greater criticism south of the border. The largely privately financed U.S. post-secondary education system has resulted in much more uneven access to high-quality learning south of the border because our institutions are essentially public sector entities that receive the vast majority of their funding from governments, provincial and federal. To be sure, the Americans, with their Harvards, Stanfords, and Princetons, have the best universities on the planet. But these are elite institutions that very few Americans ever set foot in, especially as bright young students from developing countries increasingly want and can get access to them, therefore crowding out American students. The vast majority of U.S. universities and colleges provide a much inferior education compared to these elite institutions that Canadians tend to think are the norm in America.

In Canada, with our government-financed system, we may not have any Harvards, although the University of Toronto, McGill, and Queen's are close seconds and like to think they are in this league. But on average, most of our post-secondary institutions are as good as if not better than the majority of their American counterparts. Canada is fortunate to have a relatively good and accessible education system that can provide our people with the skills and education that are required to prosper in a knowledge-based economy.

That is the good news. Now for the bad. Deep cuts by both provincial and federal governments to post-secondary education funding over the past decade are not helping the situation. Since education levels around the world are rising along with increasing globalization and technology use, the quality of Canadian schooling will not only have to be kept high but will have to improve if the country wants to succeed in the global economy. As the Dalhousie economists point out, "Canadians have become accustomed to earning wages well above the international average, and would like this fortunate situation to continue. In order for it to do so, *Canadians will have to offer skills that are similarly above the international average*" or we will inevitably lose our ability to compete in the knowledge intensive industries of the future.[19] In practice, this means Canada will have to improve the existing post-secondary educational infrastructure, which has declined in quality and accessibility in recent years, due largely to federal and provincial policy decisions.

BRING THE FEDS BACK IN

Unfortunately, the academic consensus on the importance of human capital development has not been shared by Canada's politicians. For the past few years, government funding for education has been regarded, both in Ottawa and in the provincial capital, as an area that must contribute its share or more to the deficit fight. For example, as noted in Chapter Three above, Martin's 1995 budget dumped EPF, a specific federal-provincial transfer program that had existed for nearly twenty years and pumped over $6 billion into post-secondary education in its last year of operation.[20] To be fair, the program had a major design flaw in that it did not give Ottawa the necessary stick to make sure that provinces used the cash for education. But it at least represented a political commitment by the federal government to post-secondary financing.

By contrast, the transfer that replaced EPF, the CHST, is regarded in Ottawa and the provinces as money that is largely earmarked for health care, although again the provinces are essentially free to allocate the funding as they like. For instance, the federal government wants the much-trumpeted $11.5 billion increase to the CHST, announced in 1999, to be dedicated to health care alone and expects the provinces to follow suit, largely on the basis of a letter from the premiers that commits them to use this money for health.

A cynic might conclude that Ottawa was trying to eliminate its role in post-secondary education funding when it brought in the CHST and that federal-provincial transfers would now be confined to health care. After all, the dollar amount cut out of the transfers with the advent of the CHST strangely equals the $6 billion Ottawa sent to the provinces under the old EPF program. This is not the kind of signal Ottawa should be sending to provinces or citizens about the importance of education in the knowledge economy.

Ottawa has also been actively getting out of the skills training business and leaving that to the provinces. Interestingly, this has been done over the strenuous objections of Chrétien's own Ontario caucus, who do not want "Mike the Knife" Harris to get his hands on these important policy levers. The government has been moving out of this area as part of a hasty and ill-conceived post-1995-referendum strategy to appease Quebec, which has always wanted total control over its own labour market. In the end, the devolution may not be bad, as economists are divided on the wisdom of total provincial control over labour market programming. However, add onto the federal downloading the fact that Ottawa is providing less money for education and training than in the past, and you have a recipe for future trouble.

Ottawa's de-emphasis on education and training, notwithstanding the so-called education budget of 1998, which included $1.2 billion of new investment, is short-sighted, driven by fiscal pressures and jurisdictional squabbles. Overall, the strategy betrays a misunderstanding of the economic changes that have been under way for years now. There are significant social and economic benefits that justify the subsidization of higher education, more today than in the past, and Ottawa has a key role here due to greater fiscal muscle. As Reich says, a knowledgeable and skilled workforce will attract global money to a country. Otherwise, investors can be lured only by relatively low wages and falling taxes, neither of which is realistically on Canada's horizon, despite calls from brain-dead right-wing voices who view income tax cuts as the panacea that will solve all of Canada's economic ills. Yet, even during the 1980s, before major spending restraint measures kicked in, real post-secondary education expenditures per student fell by 15 percent for universities and 9 to 10 percent for community colleges in Canada.[21] And the situation has become worse during the 1990s.

Ottawa clearly needs to get back into the post-secondary education game in a major way to stop the trend of recent years towards less government subsidization of higher education, the key economic and social consequence of which is a reduction in access to the system, as the universities and colleges increase student fees to compensate for lack of government funding (university tuition fees alone have doubled since the mid-1980s). Jurisdictional excuses for not increasing funding in such a critical policy area, in which the feds have been heavily involved before through their spending power, are simply not good enough any more and show an abdication of responsibility on Ottawa's part. As Tom Kent, one of the founders of Canada's social programs, astutely observed, "The original authors of the Constitution intended the federal government to be responsible for economic policy, but they did not understand education to be part of it."[22] In addition, the public wants Ottawa to be active in this area. Recent polls commissioned by the federal government indicate that 86 percent of Canadians think Ottawa should be doing more to make education affordable, and support for such initiatives is even higher in Quebec, which should put paid to some of the inevitable jurisdictional excuses for failing to act in this area.[23]

GOING FORWARD

In the new economy, everyone has to begin to think differently about education, higher learning, and skills training, and come to view these as fundamental economic assets rather than fiscal drags. These are not programs to be grudgingly supported as a sop to raccoon-coated, Spengler-reading elites of a century ago. If you want a productive economy you are going to need lots and lots of students churning through the education system every year, and this costs a lot of money, which many families don't have; hence the role for government. Without this shift in mindset, Canada will not have a proper debate about improving our educational infrastructure and consequently enhancing our economic prospects for the long term.

NINE

PUSHING POLICIES
FOR THE NEXT CENTURY

"In the new economy, the prospect for sustained growth will increasingly depend on 'social' innovation — changes in our institutions, policies, and practices."[1]

Political eras do not change because populations are silly or bored with the existing system. Nor do people usually turn their backs on traditions because superhumanly clever politicians have tricked them. Unfortunately, many commentators believe that the electorate is made from clay, ready to be moulded by whatever political backroom crowd has the best spin doctors, media trainers, and pollsters. Such thinking is snotty and illogical.

It is inconsistent to believe that elected officials could, on the one hand, understand nothing about the economy when it comes to, say, the effect of high tax rates and, on the other, be so subtle as to be undetectable in their treachery when it comes to winning elections.

Stupidity is not a very satisfactory explanation of political shifts. Most of the time, nations take right or left turns because they lack something. Often they face a political or economic crisis with no clear way out. Or they see stark limits to what the current crowd is proposing.

Germany in the late 1920s and early '30s is the classic example of crisis change. Here, the usually sober-thinking Germans leaped knowingly into the arms of Adolf Hitler and his twisted philosophy partly in a desperate attempt to find a way out of the Depression — not to mention their recent memory of nightmarish runaway inflation.

British voters saw weaknesses in Winston Churchill's post-war agenda and elected the Labour leader Clement Attlee. It seemed they were more interested in Attlee's plans for the future than Churchill's high-sounding rhetoric about the past.

Often, newspaper columnists and analysts make the mistake of assuming silliness or folly is why liberal or conservative regimes get into office. The electorate just does not see the truth, goes the argument. If they did, they would not have put this group of crooks into office. So politicians, cheque books at the ready, are always set to buy off voters or appeal to their grubbier instincts to get elected.

That kind of thinking is wrong. People, not politicians, pick a society's path. They may act irrationally in choosing a particular side. But the decision is based upon some reason, not usually upon on mass illusion. This is what has led many Canadians to pick conservative governments or programs during the past two decades. The economy was faltering. Politicians, relying upon earlier thinking, looked worn-out. Right-wing policies filled a void and offered answers.

The same logic applied when Canada's conservatives lost power. The economy was in trouble and the only answers this crowd had were more of the same. The siren call of more cuts was no longer winning as many converts.

Now, the Liberals in Ottawa are approaching the same point in their second mandate. The one goal the Chrétien government had, eliminating the deficit, has been achieved. But unemployment remains high, people are cranky about the current level of taxation they face, and voters still question the soundness of the country's economy.

Filling the void from the right wing is Manning's Reform Party and provincial governments such as the one in Ontario. Even so, as discussed at the beginning of this book, such politicians are retreating from their policies and sliding back into the centre.

The federal NDP has vacated the left side, hurt by internal quarrelling and a view among voters that the party is irrelevant. Instead, progressive writers, like Linda McQuaig, are either pushing non-starters, such as the Tobin Tax on speculative financial transactions, or calling for higher taxes on the wealthy, a policy for which most voters, rich or poor, appear to have little appetite.

THE ART OF THE POSSIBLE

At this crucial point in the country's public policy, the achievable, not the ideal, is the most important objective.

It does no good to push the undoable and then grouse when the ideal is not achieved. It may have given Cold Warriors a good feeling to know that Joseph Stalin was a murderer. But nothing useful stemmed from that view. Instead, it was the grubby dealmakers, such as Harry Hopkins, who kept a disastrous nuclear war from breaking out between the U.S. and the USSR and set the eventual conditions for the American victory in the critical struggle between these superpowers.

The same type of logic can be applied to Canadian economics. It might be interesting to fight the wars over government spending again or squawk about the need to dampen down currency speculation. But those debates will not lead to new policy, only to the resurrecting of old neocon warhorses, like the Fraser Institute's Michael Walker, waving their pens like swords to fend off the liberal hordes. In terms of real issues affecting real people, forget this. Go for the practical.

Here's where we get to play prime minister. In the two previous chapters, we have sketched out the basic framework for a new agenda to help move Canada into the twenty-first century knowledge economy. Here are some ideas, some borrowed, some not, that fit into this scheme.

We believe the options are politically saleable and affordable, if Ottawa gets its priorities right and makes some strategic choices. We are sticking to federal policy, the place where the big decisions are generally made and where the government can show some leadership. But as we put the emphasis on Ottawa, it must be remembered that the provinces have key roles to play, especially in primary and secondary education.

TAXES PROBABLY DON'T MATTER MUCH

One conclusion from Canadian politics in 1999 is that the federal government should ignore the idea of raising taxes to pay for some new demand-stimulating programs. That bit of Keynesianism appears dead politically and only serves to give conservative commentators another straw man to attack.

Besides, heads of government from Harris to Chrétien to Toronto mayor Mel Lastman have pretty well sworn off any kind of general tax hike. The backroom types long ago decided that that strategy was a big vote-loser. Wasting energy and political capital trying to persuade people to accept a tax increase, except in a limited form, such as for environmental purposes, might be fun. In the end, however, that program would be pointless and self-defeating.

Equally moribund is the tax-cutting revolt. Papers like the *National Post* have their e-mail systems working overtime with people outraged that Martin's removal of the high income surtax in the 1999 budget was all the tax relief he was willing to give. This is the same crowd, however, who voted Reform, who do not see the need for a proper social safety net, and who probably believe the Supreme Court's "No Means No" decision last February was a feminist plot to neuter good old boys who have a better understanding of the female psyche than women themselves.

Anyway, the tax-cutters have little economic theory to back up their calls for lower rates. They hint at some kind of supply-side response from these reductions but never quite come out and say it lest they become the objects of ridicule.

The tax-cut frenzy is an expression of an understandable annoyance at years of paying taxes with little to show. Essentially, these people are the embodiment of the "give me back my money" protesters, people who are tired of watching their tax dollars going down the drain. They want their money and they do not really care whether or not such refunds would cause economic damage.

That leaves the advocates, like Ontario's Harris, to maintain that such reductions boost consumer spending.

Fifty years ago, they might have had a case. Their interests and the general interests of the Canadian economy were in closer alignment. In the industrial age, consumer demand was much more important and exports were less crucial to the country's well-being. Thus one could make a case that cutting tax rates and getting money back into the hands of individual Canadians would be an important step towards economic recovery.

The information highway and the global economy have changed all that. Canada experienced a recovery after the 1991 recession that was essentially based upon export markets. As the Asian countries ran into trouble in 1998, domestic consumer demand did kick in to keep the Canadian economy rolling.

That type of spending, however, is driven by consumer confidence, not tax rates. If people believe they will have a job for the foreseeable future and that their economic prospects will improve as well, they are more likely to boost their purchases. Governments would have to make such a large tax cut to increase real purchasing power that it would put at risk either budget-balancing or needed social programs, if the economy hit a downturn.

A case can be made for small scale tax reductions, but not the deep cuts contemplated by supporters of this policy. In fact, in the 1999 Ontario election, Harris did not even try to use economic logic to sell his 20 percent tax cut. He just appealed directly to voters' wallets.

Ottawa would be better off trying to ensure that everyone who wanted one has a well-paying job. Then, more people would spend more money over a longer period of time.

WHAT THE FIRM LOCATES WHERE IS CRUCIAL

Tax rates have been less important than in the past because firms now divide up their operations more than ever before. Nortel Networks Inc. has research facilities in Toronto and North Carolina and production plants in Dallas and Calgary. Ford has assembly lines in Ontario and Quebec, the United States, and Brazil. Firms now have research facilities located in different countries than their head offices, which may in turn be continents away from where they build the plants.

In rare cases, firms may have trouble getting high-priced talent and cite taxes as the cause. Nortel has complained about this. Search experts, however, point out that the opportunities to advance in leading-edge industries are often greater south of the border, pushing taxes down the list of reasons to leave.

These days, most companies are interested in the lowest costs and highest production locations for all their operations. But each separate part of the company will emphasize different sides of the cost-productivity coin. Knocking off bits of plastic into toys or trinkets is probably best left to low-wage Asian nations, such as China and Vietnam. Our better standards of living dictate higher salaries than such industries are usually willing to fork over.

Canada might do better to chase the work designing the plastic bangles. Here, a college degree and an ingrained ability to innovate are more important than a cheap wage rate. We should try to be competitive in those parts of a company that value clever brains to make better products, as opposed to having the stamina to remain at a sewing machine for thirteen hours a day for a pittance.

SOCIAL PROGRAMS AS ECONOMIC ASSETS

Once Ottawa rejects the tax-cutting or tax-raising arguments, the government needs to recognize that well-designed social programs are key economic assets.

For too long, politicians and various commentators have treated things like medicare, welfare policy, and education as if these programs were largesse to be given to the masses by a benevolent wealthy elite. As a result, some thinkers have often looked at these pieces of the social safety net as something to be chopped when times became tough.

Far from being economic drains on Canada, universal health care, education, and welfare all have strong underlying economic justifications and help us to be competitive. Pushing such logic publicly, rather than tapping into the electorate's discontent with these programs, might be a better way for governments to develop valuable voter support for keeping these programs.

EDUCATION

Governments of all stripes have decided to raise tuition and other costs for post-secondary education at the very point in our historical development when getting a degree, any kind of degree, is crucial to future employment prospects. Good public policy would dictate that the opposite is needed. Ottawa and the provinces should lower the costs of entering a university on the assumption that we need more, not fewer, productive and innovative workers.

This is not an equity question, not a matter of being fair to young people. It is an issue of economic survival. Without enough college and university graduates, Canada is not going to be productive enough to remain competitive in the knowledge-based economy. The country already lacks the prerequisite number of computer programmers and other software types.

As Quebec industrialist Charles Sirois has said: "A recent study by one of Canada's leading high-technology companies showed that the 175 Canadian technology companies planned to hire 10,000 people in 1998. The most recent data available indicates that all of the country's computer science and electrical engineering programs combined to produce less than 5,000 undergraduates."[2] Raising the financial entry bar for access to institutions where these skills are learned seems to be a strange way to go into the next century.

HEALTH CARE

The same can be said for Canada's universal health care system. After more than thirty years in service, the national medicare set-up is creaky and in need of extensive repair. The country, however, has a gold mine in this system. Time after time, companies such as the car makers cite the money they save by not having to establish employee medical insurance schemes as one of the biggest factors in favour of locating in this country.

Besides that benefit, the country's universal health care system provides another helping hand to the economy. Under our system, Canadian workers are healthier than they would otherwise be, especially among lower-wage employees. With a U.S.-style pay-as-you-go system, people might ration their use of medical services in the same way they would any other product or service, by price, not need. The point is not whether Canadian workers are more physically fit than their American counterparts, just that they would be worse off under a privately funded system.

In Canada, anyone can get medical attention as often as he or she wants. Perhaps this system is not the most efficient from the viewpoint of matching the price of a service to its demand. If you think of medical services as maximizing the number of healthy people, however, then it is better than the free market variation. Thus, the Canadian economy gets a healthier workforce with less time off. More people in the workplace rather than at home sounds like a route to a productive country.

WELFARE

Finally, and the toughest sell of all, Canada needs to reinforce its welfare and unemployment insurance systems to make sure recipients are able to get necessary training, child care, health care, and other essentials to become effective employees.

For the past fifteen years or so, the debate has revolved around the alleged need to cut payments to motivate the unemployed and those in penury to get jobs. And that argument has hinged on the assumption that many of these people would rather get a small amount of social assistance and not look for work than spend the time trying to become gainfully employed.

These groups, like everyone else, need to get the proper skills to enter the difficult labour markets of the next years. In past decades, it probably made sense to give social assistance recipients a kick in the pants to make sure they were trying to find work. Back then, entry-level jobs were plentiful and employment requirements more likely than not consisted of whether you could breathe and were not legally blind.

In the 1990s, employers ask for university degrees as the prerequisite for many jobs. And those few "ports of entry" positions, such as in hotels and restaurants, usually are not the high-growth information-highway-type employment people seek. Shoving a welfare recipient into one of these jobs would almost always mean a slow move up the employment ladder, if at all.

Canada is better off spending a bit of extra money on additional training and daycare now, in order to get such people on the correct career path. In the knowledge economy, expecting these groups to make their way by themselves into high-value-added jobs on their own is silly. They will need help if they are to stay off the welfare rolls and out of the unemployment lines. And such assistance will be cheaper at the beginning of their working lives rather than a decade or so later.

Does this mean spending more money on these shiftless souls? Perhaps. Hence, changes to federal and provincial tax codes that do not take all of their social assistance payments away from them the minute they enter the workforce would make sense; so would programs like the American earned income tax credit, a variant of which is now being pursued in the U.K.

Workfare is not important from an economic perspective. The theory is that welfare recipients need a connection to the workplace to get a better job. Too often, however, the tasks these people do under these programs are manual labour. Workfare gets them no useful training or employment prospects. Instead, they just waste their time when they could at least be receiving training for a job with some real future prospects.

A mandatory program that would make more sense is one that Harris has suggested, placing social assistance types in high school classes or training rooms. That way they would still be forced to do something in return for their welfare cheque, satisfying conservatives, and would improve their skills, making them at least marginally more employable.

Making social programs into economic assets fits the Reich scheme. He has argued that countries will be competitive only if their workforces are efficient, healthy, and well-trained. A worker in a Third World country will not be able to exhibit any of these assets when he or she faces a crumbling social infrastructure.

In Canada, some of our social programs are a huge advantage in making a competitive workforce. Keeping health and education systems that are accessible and world-class is crucial to giving everyone a shot at becoming productive members of the new information-intensive world.

ROMER'S INFORMATION HIGHWAY

If Reich's theory focuses on human capital, Romer's emphasizes technology and innovation. His increasing returns to scale idea implies that

Ottawa and the provinces maintain a strong hand in the development of the country's scientific infrastructure. Falling behind in this race almost guarantees you will lose.

Ottawa's policy, begun by John Manley, to get the Internet into Canada's schools should be commended and continued. That will expose students to a research and learning tool that will only become more important in the future.

As with other policies, however, the provinces should not use the appearance of the Internet as an excuse to cut services, such as the old-fashioned school library. Instead of exposing the child to more ways of learning, such funding reductions could wind up giving the boy or girl fewer opportunities to undertake research projects than before the advent of the Internet.

As well, all levels of government need to find ways to ensure that children in lower-income areas who attend less-modern schools receive the equipment and expertise to tap into the information highway. Often, policies that are designed to be equal across all schools fail because students in wealthier areas get access to better computers and they have parents who have a more complete understanding of the medium and money with which to buy the best at-home gear. The poorer kids get left in the dust, trying to make do in a more difficult learning environment with inferior equipment.

Less well-to-do kids will be behind the educational eight ball if governments do not take up some leadership to make sure they can get access to modern learning tools. This becomes even more important because students are likely to use an increasing number of multimedia devices to learn more things.

Outlining the need for equal opportunity is one thing. Finding ways of delivering it is something else. Corporations might help. They already have a productivity incentive to ensure that kids who might end up on their plant floors have the proper skill set. And helping them receive this learning in school is more cost-effective than getting them to take remedial training on the job.

What Ottawa and the provinces could offer is a charity tax credit for equipment and employee time spent in Canada's poorer schools. The company might donate terminals and other gear and the time of their employees to train teachers and students. Firms already write off monies given to a variety of charities. Adding another deduction to the list is not too onerous a cost for governments to incur in return for better-educated students in the country's less wealthy districts.

In a similar vein, Ottawa needs to figure out ways to bring the information infrastructure in all provinces up to standard. Communication systems are competitive advantages in the new economy, and the federal government should make sure that places like Prince Edward Island and Newfoundland as well as Alberta and Ontario have good infrastructure.

This is the regional development program of the future. Rather than throwing good federal money after bad by propping up dying industries and failing firms, Ottawa should be using its subsidy mechanisms to help build the information infrastructure in the "have-not" regions to help firms in these provinces become more competitive.

Unfortunately, Ottawa's regional development agencies continue to operate in an outdated manner oriented towards business subsidies,[3] often on the basis of political criteria. This approach has not served these regions or the Canadian taxpayers well over the years and has led most economists to pronounce the regional development programs to be almost a total waste of money and effort. A new approach that focuses on the infrastructure of the future could, however, make a big difference to struggling economies.

BLINDED BY SCIENCE

Ottawa also has to keep its hand in the area of pure science. The country needs to develop basic research to lay the groundwork for subsequent, more commercially oriented innovation by private sector firms. Governments frequently fund such scientific work since individual firms often have little incentive to make these expenditures on their own. If Canada is falling behind in pure science, then Ottawa should step in on the grounds that Canada cannot afford to falter in creating the proper conditions for an innovative economy.

Despite a recent funding increase, however, the Chrétien government still only supports the Natural Sciences and Engineering Research Council, the government's primary science funding instrument, at 1994 levels. Much more needs to be done to build pure science capacity in Canada and stop the drain of Canada's top science graduates to the U.S., where larger government funding for science R&D is readily available.

Romer also recommends encouragement of private sector advice to universities on the best places to spend scarce research dollars. After all, these firms are the ones most likely to use the results from such work. It only makes sense that they should have some input in what projects are to be pursued.

That does not mean unleashing a flood of corporate-sponsored research chairs and company-funded studies. Such a system would likely cramp researchers' freedom to look at various projects and publicize results. As well, there is a threat that the university scientists working in these programs would merely become adjuncts to the corporation's scientific staff.

It might make more sense to set up industry-specific advisory groups as the way to channel advice and perhaps money to various researchers. The academics could pursue a project with an application across a number of companies in one sector. In this way, the universities would not be tied to particular companies and Romer's spillover effects would be institutionalized.

Now let us turn to some specifics on the human capital, or "Reichian," side of the equation. But let's start with what governments definitely should not do in this area.

INCOME CONTINGENT REPAYMENT LOANS: AN IDEA WHOSE TIME SHOULD NEVER COME

A strange thing happened in policy wonk circles in this country in recent years. Thinkers whose views span the ideological spectrum have reached a consensus on the merits of a cumbersome-sounding idea called "income contingent repayment loans" (ICR) for students.

These types talk about ICR as if it were a new cure-all for the chronic underfunding of post-secondary education that would not hamper accessibility for young Canadians. Pick up any volume on the ills of Canada's universities and you will get an eyeful about ICR. There is only one flaw in this meeting of policy minds: they are wrong.

To proceed, you will have to learn a few governmental acronyms. PSE refers to post-secondary education and CHST refers to the Canada Health and Social Transfer, Martin's new way to transfer federal money to the provinces. EPF refers to the old Established Programs Financing transfers, and CSL, a new term, refers to the Canada Student Loans program.

Let's be blunt. The ICR program is one of the wackiest ideas to come along since Art Laffer drew up his supply-side theory on the back of that napkin at Wall Street's famous Michael 1 restaurant. Yet, Canadian policy types almost universally support the concept.

Credible and knowledgeable thinkers as divergent as the public policy specialist Judith Maxwell, Liberals Tom Kent and Lloyd Axworthy,[4] the always Tory *Globe and Mail* editorial board, and the more conserv-ative Fraser and C.D. Howe Institutes are all proponents of some version of this type of loan system. The emergence of a consensus on any issue should raise eyebrows. Perhaps we should be especially skeptical in this case.

Before we start criticizing this idea, we should ask ourselves, why is almost everybody except us in favour of this concept? What do all these well-intentioned, analytical people have in common that would lead them to advocate an obviously flawed idea? The answer is that this crowd are invariably over fifty years of age and have not sat in a student's desk in a classroom for several decades. In addition, most of them were among the best students of their day, breezing through university at a time when a post-secondary education cost a fraction of what it does now and when even a bachelor's degree in philosophy could guarantee you some sort of reasonably well-paying job. Today, such a degree only guarantees you some debt and the ability to talk intelligently about Aristotle at parties.

The common trait among these thinkers who so favour the ICR plan is their unrealistic view about the average student's lot and about the problems that would stem from introducing this program. Simply put, they do not know what they are talking about.

THE BASICS

As a concept, the ICR is pretty straightforward. Fiscal pressures have resulted in both levels of government cutting post-secondary education funding significantly in recent years. Consequently, universities and community colleges, desperate for cash, have raised tuition sharply. Since 1980, tuition fees have risen by 115 percent.[5] And all sorts of extra charges have been introduced where there had been few or none.

Already, many students, especially from low-income families, cannot afford to pursue a university or college education, partly because they cannot secure enough student loan money from the current federal and provincial loan programs to pay these ever-rising fees. These students also are further discouraged because the payback period on these loans is too short; the maximum time is about ten years. That leaves the loan repayment schedule too expensive. For example, the monthly payments on a $24,000 student loan are about $350 for the next decade.

So, ICR advocates came up with a different approach to get more money into the system and into the hands of eligible students. Replace the current loan system with one in which students can borrow as much as they need to finance their education, for example, $80,000 for a four-year degree. Your repayment schedule will now be based upon your income after graduation. And the payout period can be strung out over your entire working life.

Under this model, your monthly payments wind up quite low if, say, your undergraduate arts degree gets you only a low-paying job once you finish. Hypothetically, you might pay only $100 a month on your $80,000 loan. And you would make these payments for the next half-century or so. If you retire or die before repaying the loan, the beneficent state will write off the remainder.

To anyone who has had to write an exam in the past decade, the notion that an ICR scheme will reduce the barriers for teenagers who want to go to university defies common sense. And yet these policy thinkers believe that a nineteen-year-old high school graduate will think nothing of assuming as much as $80,000 in debt to finance a bachelor's degree merely because they may only have to make a monthly payment of $100 for the rest of their working lives.

For many students it is the big number on the top of the loan appli-cation, not the little one at the bottom, that will scare them off. Many are likely to decide that borrowing such a large amount of money is too risky in proportion to the potential financial reward at the end of the degree.

In particular, the long string of zeros might be alarming to a student from a low-income family who may have shaky prospects of getting a good job upon graduation. For example, Johnny graduates with his four-year economics degree, a relatively marketable one, with a $30,000 debt. He did fine as an undergraduate and is considering graduate school. But his marks were not good enough to secure a scholarship or even a teaching assistantship to pay for his studies. What can Johnny do? According to the ICR proponents, he can take out another big loan to get his master's degree, placing his total debt a bit south of $60,000. After all, this is only going to add another $75 a month to his forty-year repayment plan. No disincentive to graduate school here, is there?

Another perverse side effect would likely be that our brightest students would opt for degree programs that hold out the highest promise of money rewards, like law or business administration. Consequently, less financially lucrative but critically important areas of study, such as science research, could suffer, an outcome not in the best long-term interests of our economy.[6] An ICR system could promote entry into paper-pushing fields like law more than innovative fields like engineering, not an outcome Romer would welcome. Then remember William F. Buckley Jr.'s quip to the effect that a few hundred of the best minds in America are wasted each year in the Harvard Law Faculty.

In the real world, students are not likely to think the way the ICR supporters expect. Typically, students will not ponder their monthly payments during their degrees, in part because the student loans administrators do not offer this information until you graduate.

Instead they will worry about their total debt load. By increasing that figure enormously, as an ICR scheme would do, many able students who could pursue post-secondary education simply would not. And those inclined towards graduate or professional study would be more likely to opt for the work world to start paying off their big loans. Many people are uncomfortable carrying huge loans even if the payments are small. They will be reluctant to take on additional financing for major purchases, such as cars or houses, until their student debt is paid off or substantially reduced.

Another concern is one of fairness between generations. Tom Courchene, a long-time policy thinker who reluctantly favours these loans, has posed this question: "Is the enthusiasm for ICR schemes related to the fact that we might be able to avoid restructuring of the existing social envelope (e.g., public pensions) by enticing the young to borrow directly (via ICR schemes) to finance their own social policy needs? I am reminded here of the *Selfish Generations? The Aging of New Zealand's Welfare State* (Thomas, D. 1991) where the theme is that New Zealand's welfare system has largely been hijacked by a single generation or cohort (the soon-to-be-golden agers). Are ICRs a way for Canada to follow suit here?"[7]

Perhaps having zipped through university on the cheap, baby boomers are now trying to avoid subsidizing the next generation's education, by advocating an ICR program where much more of the cost is borne by students. The worst thing about the ICR proposals, however, is that governments might use the system as an excuse to cut funding to universities and colleges even more. Administrations are likely to crank up tuition and other fees further because everyone will operate under the assumption that young people can borrow all the money they need to pay the costs.

In the end, the financial burden of higher learning will be shifted onto the backs of students. Some people favour this approach on the reasonable grounds that the main beneficiaries, the university attendees, should pay for most or all of their education.

Society and the economy, however, benefit greatly from a well-educated citizenry, and as we move into a knowledge-based economy this is even more important. Consequently these costs should be pooled. Governments should do more than they are doing now to subsidize post-secondary education, rather than relying upon such a program as ICR.

Interestingly, very few organized groups are stumping the ICR idea in Canada. Not even the banks like it. And only the odd provincial government, notably the Harris Conservatives, who valued learning so much they had a high school dropout in charge of the education ministry, has floated the concept. The Reform Party also likes income contingent loans because they would reduce social policy costs to free up money for tax cuts.

Although Tom Kent claims some student groups support ICR, they are not raising their hands too high.[8] That is because the ICR concept is flawed and should not be considered in a country such as Canada that is on the path towards the knowledge economy.

PSE VOUCHERS: AN IDEA WHOSE TIME IS NOW

One thing the education crowd has right is that the current system of federal student loans, the CSL program, should be scrapped. Similarly, the money being spent on Chrétien's Millennium Scholarship Program, which has laudable goals, could be put to better use by helping to fund a voucher system for post-secondary education.

Politically, it is hard to see why Ottawa, which is increasingly worried about its declining visibility across the country, would keep a program like CSL, through which the federal government subsidizes loans to students but gets no credit or visibility for this money.

Most students do not even know that Ottawa provides these kinds of loans because the provinces administer both the federal and provincial portions. For instance, in Ontario, students apply for both the provincial and federal loan programs on one application form addressed to the Ontario Ministry of Education. The money is usually transferred directly into the students' bank accounts. So they assume it comes from Queen's Park. The only time Ottawa appears is if a student defaults on a loan payment. This is not the kind of visibility the federal government should be striving for. In Ontario, all students refer to the combined provincial and federal loan program as OSAP (Ontario Student Assistance Program), not the CSL.

Here is a better way for the feds to support post-secondary education and get some political kudos for doing so. Try a new system based in part on vouchers. Ottawa dumps the current CSL and Millennium Scholarship programs and institutes a system of vouchers available to students — according to financial need — who are enrol-ling in Canadian universities or community colleges. These bits of paper would not be loans but would be equivalent to study grants.

This is not a new idea. Until the education funding crunch of a few years ago, some provinces and the federal government provided grants based on financial need that could add up to almost $5,000 per year, and Ottawa still provides modest study grants to special-needs students. The Millennium program is supposed to provide similar awards to needy students. But the voucher system, compared to cash grants, is the better, more market-oriented way to go.

The vouchers would be redeemable at any Canadian post-secondary institution for any education-related expense, such as tuition and purchases of books. The grant would only be worth something at post-secondary institutions for legitimate school needs. That would get around the problem of students using loans or cash grants for things other than education. Everyone has a story about university students who were not really interested in getting a degree but would spend their government aid on stereos or beer. The voucher proposal would eliminate these abuses because the notes would only be redeemable for school expenses on campus. This may sound paternalistic, but sometimes students need a little parenting.

The face value of the voucher could be on a sliding scale based on the student's income and the family's financial circumstances, as is the case with existing student loan programs. All needy students would be eligible for voucher support, not a fixed and arbitrary number of students, as is the case with the Millennium Scholarships.

For Ottawa to be in this game in any significant way the maximum value of the vouchers would have to be in the range of at least $5,000 annually, and this money could be supplemented with provincial student loans and personal savings. The federal government would get great visibility for the program because a voucher with appropriate CANADA logos and labelled with a catchy acronym — FSSP for Federal Student Support Program, perhaps — would be handed to each needy student to support them.

This idea might come under fire from provincial governments, notably Quebec, because of their jurisdiction over education. The constitutional barrier, however, could be crossed. Parents and students in Quebec or any other province do not have much time for whining about which level of government should be providing grants to students to help them cope with increased school costs that are due, in part, to funding cuts by the provincial governments themselves. The golden rule of fiscal federalism, which voters seem to support, is that he who provides the gold sets the rules. Besides, even if there is some minor national unity fallout, so what?[9] Ottawa needs to be in this area for the good of our economy and should be prepared to take a little heat.

Admittedly, a voucher system will cost significant cash and will not do much to contain the rising costs of tuition and other fees. Ottawa, however, should be spending more on education and has the necessary funds if it could get its economic priorities right. If Ottawa needs more money for the program than is made available by scrapping the CSL and Millennium Scholarships, the federal government might want to consider removing that portion of the CHST cash transfer that is supposed to be for post-secondary education, and use the money to pay for vouchers. Unfortunately, no one, including Ottawa, has a clue how much of the CHST is being or should be used for education.

So how much do we remove? One way around this problem would be to take out the portion of the CHST equal to the previous EPF education cash component that was folded into the CHST in 1995 and was worth about $6 billion when EPF was scrapped.[10] That would mean that all federal educational transfers were being used for education for the first time in decades. Such an approach, admittedly radical, would seem to contradict the spirit of the Social Union Framework Agreement that the federal government signed with the provinces this year. Hence, it is not our preferred funding option for political reasons. But if money is the only stumbling block, this approach should be considered.

A NEW FEDERAL PSE TRANSFER

As should be obvious by now, we hold the minority view that Ottawa must play a key role in post-secondary education in Canada. The voucher proposal is the first component of a two-part agenda for Ottawa that should be implemented.

The second component is a new per capita federal financial transfer to provinces for the express purpose of funding universities and colleges. This can get directly at the funding problem that universities and community colleges face and that students are bearing the brunt of through increased PSE costs. It amounts to bringing the feds back into post-secondary education financing in a major way.

Despite the decentralist mindset that dominates Ottawa today, there is a more compelling rationale for federal involvement in education now than there was in the days when we had an earmarked federal transfer for such purposes.

We could try a transfer somewhat like the old EPF arrangement with an added twist. Under EPF, a block grant was transferred to the provinces, part of which was to be used for education. A basic design flaw in this set-up, however, was that there was no way for Ottawa to make sure the money actually filtered down to the colleges and universities. Under our proposal — let's call it the Federal Education Equality Transfer (FEET) — Ottawa would provide to the provinces a per capita amount of cash with some kind of an inflation escalator to be used only for funding colleges and universities.

The Social Union agreement requires the federal government to get majority provincial support for such a measure. We do not think that this would be an insurmountable challenge, since provinces know better than anyone that the education system needs more money and recently have been urging Ottawa to put more money into PSE in the aftermath of the health care cash infusion.

As well, the premiers are sensitive to the fact that their electorates want more resources pumped into this area. To make sure the new money is used for its intended purpose, Ottawa would get the provinces to sign an accord (not unlike the one the premiers put pen to for the recent health care grant) committing provincial governments to use this new money for PSE.

The accord would have to be non-binding for the provinces to sign it. But our suggestion is not as foolish as it looks. You might think it naïve to expect that a commitment with no penalties attached would be enough to ensure the money would go to post-secondary education. However, the political consequences for failing to honour such a commitment could be severe, given the high level of public support for more government funding of PSE and the cuts of recent years.

The well-organized college and university lobby would watch closely to make sure that the provinces were transferring the federal money to them, and this would act as a powerful accountability mechanism to guard against provincial backsliding. This approach would improve funding and access to the education system and would be a political winner for the federal government, assuming, of course, that they can get the provinces to buy into the idea. A transfer in the range of $3 billion to $4 billion annually, well under the EPF education component, would be a good start.

"REVOLVING" TRAINING

After the breathtakingly close 1995 referendum result, Ottawa relented on a long-standing Quebec demand by giving the provinces full jurisdiction and control over "manpower" training, or labour market development programming (e.g., government-supported skills training programming).

The federal government promised to give labour market programming to every province, not just Quebec, so they would look like good symmetrical federalists and not antagonize other provinces and "equality of the provinces" federalists. Currently, labour market development agreements to give the provinces these powers have been signed with all provinces except Ontario.

This approach leaves a lot to be desired. Ottawa needs to be

re-involved in labour market programming. And hence we are proposing some "revolving," as opposed to devolving, of training to Ottawa.
These proposals, however, are not overly inconsistent with the current
labour market development agreements. As a result, they should
encounter only minor jurisdictional problems. These changes do not
preclude the federal government from finishing their decentralist
magnum opus by signing a labour market agreement with Ontario.

Experience tells us that Ottawa is not particularly good at providing
effective training. This was another reason for the drive towards devolution to the provinces, which allegedly are somewhat better at it
(although the evidence for that is scant).[11]

Conversely, employer-based training is quite effective and usually
superior to that provided by governments, in part because firms have a
financial, or bottom-line, incentive to do it right. For example, Canada's
banks basically train all their staff and, as a result, require fewer formal
educational requirements than you might think.

Ottawa could encourage more companies to train their workers
through a company-based training tax deduction. The concept is simple enough. Firms that demonstrated that they provided some degree
of formal training to an existing employee (not a new one) over some
extended period, say six months, would be eligible for a tax deduction.

To be sure, there would be administrative hurdles to jump, such as
how to prevent firms from claiming that every time they give an
employee some new task to do they qualify for a tax deduction. Such
obstacles should not stop Ottawa trying to encourage more employer-
based training through such a mechanism.

Another federal training initiative worth considering, which also
has limited jurisdictional fallout, was a proposal recently floated by the
Toronto lawyer Raymond Koskie, on behalf of several Ontario-based
construction trade unions. The Ontario construction industry pays

for worker training through contributions, from both employers and employees, to trust funds, which are drawn upon to pay for training during down-periods in the industry. The objective is to keep a workforce that is up-to-date on the latest technology. These training trust funds have been around for years, and in the past Ottawa has contributed some money to them. Several years ago, however, the federal government got out of this particular subsidization game.

Now, Koskie wants the federal government to get back into this through a cost-sharing arrangement. In this case, the construction industry would contribute 70 percent to the trust funds and Ottawa 30 percent. This idea makes sense because, again, the training is employer-based and there is an incentive for the employer to do it right and efficiently.

But Ottawa can play an important role in encouraging even more employer training by topping up these trust funds and creating an incentive for other sectors to establish them. In addition, this program does not look too expensive. Indeed, Koskie estimated a program open to all interested sectors would initially cost about $100 million a year.[12] Or the federal government could simply cap the annual amount available at a certain limit, promoting a first-come-first-served system (admittedly not an ideal approach). So far, though, Koskie's efforts have fallen on deaf ears due to jurisdictional concerns of over-sensitive bureaucrats and politicians in the nation's capital.

WORK AND THE FAMILY IN THE TWENTY-FIRST CENTURY

Canada's newspapers and business magazines lately have become fixated on the country's productivity performance. This hysteria has led to calls for alleged panaceas such as broad-based income tax cuts to improve performance in this area. Lost in the debate is the fact that, regardless of our productivity performance, many Canadians are working longer and harder than ever before.

As a result, child-rearing, part of the essence of what Galbraith called the Good Society, has suffered as both parents trot off to work at seven in the morning and often return twelve hours later. In many people's minds, striving for greater productivity translates into working even longer and harder. This is the nature of our new economy and there is not much that government can do about it.

The state, however, can play a critical role in ensuring that the kids of these working families receive the proper care during their crucial formative years through highly trained, licensed, regulated, and professional child caregivers. There is nothing new here of course. The federal Tories in the 1980s and the Liberals ten years later recognized the need for government-funded child care. In both cases, however, nothing ever came of it.

Re-examining a national daycare system or some sort of child care support would inevitably get caught up in federal-provincial squabbling. Nevertheless, the goal of good child care is too important to be stopped by internecine government warfare, which the public does not understand or have much time for. Instead of engaging in frustrating and likely fruitless intergovernmental negotiations on a cost-shared program, Ottawa could use its undisputed jurisdiction over tax policy to help fund decent child care.

In fact the feds already do this through a child care tax deduction that can be quite significant in value for well-off families, as much as a $3,000 tax saving per child. This instrument, however, is of less value to families at the low end of the income scale simply because they have little, if any, tax from which to deduct such expenses. As a result, many working Canadians who need daycare are often forced to select poorer quality care, which often amounts to little more than babysitting.

If Canada expects to have a well-trained population in the coming generations, this kind of inequity is unacceptable. It is not sufficient to ensure the intellectual development of children so that they can rise above the income and education levels of their parents and prosper in the knowledge economy. Leaving the present system in place may limit the potential of these kids, given what we know today about the critical importance of the first few years of a child's life to long-term intellectual development.

As Tom Kent has pointed out, "The irony, in short, is that much as we talk about the importance of education and investment in people, as a society we are probably on balance doing no more, perhaps less, for the early development of our children than was done a generation or two ago."[13] Moreover, many of our major European competitors do more than Canada in establishing the public services necessary to contribute to proper child development.

Ottawa has a responsibility to provide more funding for this purpose, especially at the low-income end. And, here, Kent has advocated a reasonable proposal, suggesting the conversion of the existing child care tax deduction into a refundable tax credit. This money would be a payment to individuals similar to the refundable GST tax credit. Because the deduction would be calculated on your tax form, the credit would be an income-tested social benefit. The full benefit of the government payment would go to poorer Canadians with payments decreasing as incomes rise and no payment at a specified income threshold.

The credit would operate like a voucher and would only be redeemable at child care centres that passed some standard of care, as set and regulated by the provinces. The payment could be issued monthly or quarterly so that federal visibility, always important, would be high.

Provincial co-operation in administering such a program would be important but not essential. If daycare tax credit funding is provided by Ottawa, demand will likely over time create a supply of well-run and effective child care centres that would be eligible for such funding, regardless of provincial assistance.

This type of initiative fits into Canada's knowledge economy framework in two ways.

First, it recognizes Canada's economy is composed mainly of families in which both parents work. And they need help in rearing their children.

Second, early investment in child care is the first and most basic human capital investment for governments. Good care now will have a profound effect on an individual's educational and intellectual achievements down the road. Reasonable child care helps set out the road map for future human capital development in the knowledge economy. In short, good social policy is good economics.

THE NEED FOR DEBATE

As the saying goes, the longest journey begins with a single step. Our policy ideas are not meant as a binding blueprint to be applied by a government. Instead, they are gentle nudges, designed to get the public policy going in the proper direction. The hope is that other, better thinkers than we will apply themselves to this task and get the debate going concerning the best ways to advance this economic framework for the coming liberal era.

AFTERWORD

Turn out the light. Bolt the barn door. Let the fat lady sing. Use whatever cliché you like. But Canada's hard-right conservative era is over. Their shining moment was in the early to middle part of this decade, when Manning appeared on the edge of a national breakthrough. Harris had just taken power in Ontario and Klein was increasingly popular in Alberta. And people seemed ready for a good dose of market reform and spending reductions, in both of which these parties excel.

Five years later, however, fears of a right-wing sweep in Canada have proven to be unfounded. Manning is a spent force and both Harris and Klein have inched back to the political centre. They have jumped, or been pushed, off their policy platform largely because the main theme driving their agenda, the huge deficits of the '80s and '90s, has disappeared.

Pretty well every country and province was leaking red ink at the start of the '90s. A couple of years later and the deficits have gone in most provinces and in Ottawa. Governments now have the happy task of deciding where to spend the growing surpluses. People have a harder time accepting stringent fiscal medicine when there is money in the public coffers to spend.

Also, Canada is quickly becoming an information, rather than resource or manufacturing, economy. In that world, the neoconservatives who dominated the past twenty years have nothing to say.

Their message is about maintaining control when the government is spending too much money, and when people look to such administrations for a simple way out of a current economic bind. In a forward-looking time, when governments have to marshal resources for new infra-structure and when the underlying principles of the economy are no longer clear, conservatives can only talk about the invisible hand and the need to keep the faith.

Voters and taxpayers want to move into the next industrial era but are reluctant to accept that progress depends on the whim of a Walrasian auctioneer or some other market-based economist's construct. They need a government that appears engaged and ready to pursue policies to get Canada to the next stage. A quick survey across this land tells one that a public policy vacuum exists in Canada.

A number of liberal to left-wing writers, such as Linda McQuaig, James Laxer, and Brooke Jeffery, have talked about the need to defeat Canada's right-wing agenda. To these analysts, this country remains in a titanic ideological struggle for the hearts and minds of voters.

We believe that fight is over. For better or worse, governments and voters have adopted some aspects of the conservative program, namely balancing budgets. Other parts, such as private health care, have already died.

It is time to move. Fighting the inflationary battle of the early '90s is for old soldiers, not new thinkers. People are ready for the next stage. But no one is stepping forward to offer much.

In an attempt to fill this vacuum, this volume has outlined a program that is workable, not ridiculously expensive, one that still operates in free markets. These policies would build upon the attributes of the country's workforce to make Canada one of the most productive economies on the planet. We also have suggested ways to get Canadians, too many of whom are still unemployed, ready for the new knowledge-based work of the twenty-first century.

These suggestions, however, are just that. They are not designed as a comprehensive list. Instead, they are put out in the hope that analysts and economists who may have kept quiet during the right-wing ascendancy of recent history will come forward with their own ideas of the proper role of an activist government.

Politicians can continue to pursue conservative policies in a bid to make Canada's economy even more market-oriented. But these thinkers have little strength left in the public policy arena. Much like their liberal predecessors, their ideas are stale. Instead, they get attention mainly by the volume of their voices rather than the quality of their thinking.

Although there is a policy black hole in Ottawa and the provinces, the next group of idea men and women that walk through the door will not win by default. People who advocate a better view of government have to devise clever policies that move the economy down the path of strong growth and productivity improvement without returning Canada to the days of high deficits and excessive government regulation.

Liberal academics must realize that, in the new world, inflation and the size of your borrowing matter. And government has less ability to establish rules to induce particular kinds of behaviour. Reich and Romer are important because they recognize that the traditional approaches to economic management no longer apply in the information age.

Instead, governments need to work to develop the skills of the country's workforce and ensure that these people and corporations have the tools with which to be productive forces in the next century.

You could go back to a former era when Ottawa tried to control the economy through legislative rules and large subsidies. A return to these long-forgotten policies would only make Canada a laughingstock among international investors and would be a menace to anyone in this country who has a job or savings.

Instead, Canadians need a running shot at getting and keeping a job in the next decade. And all groups, rich and poor, need a place at the economic table. That way, the Canadian economy will end up being increasingly productive with higher-paying jobs and better prospects. In a country currently beset with deep-seated economic uncertainty, that's not such a bad outcome.

NOTES

INTRODUCTION: GROPING TOWARDS THE NEW LIBERALISM

1   Conversation with authors.

ONE: THE LONG MARCH OF THE NEOCONS

1   Patrick Dunleavy and Brendan O'Leary, *Theories of the State: The Politics of Liberal Democracy* (London: Macmillan, 1987).

2.   For more on the effects of the Mulroney government's de-indexation of tax brackets and credits (which has been retained under the Liberals), see Finn Poschmann, "Inflated Taxes, Deflated Paycheques," C.D. Howe Institute, *Commentary*, no. 118, Dec. 1998, and Ken Battle, *No Taxation Without Indexation* (Ottawa: Caledon Institute of Social Policy, 1998).

3   Tom Flanagan, *Waiting for the Wave: The Reform Party and Preston Manning* (Toronto: Stoddart, 1995).

4   Flanagan, *Waiting for the Wave*, p. 41.

5   Today Grubel, who retired from politics in 1997, is spearheading an emerging debate, along with economists Tom Courchene and Richard Harris, on the merits of a common North American currency.

6   The most notable efforts at fiscal containment undertaken by the Tories were partial de-indexation of the income tax system, the ending of universality in family allowances and old age pensions, cuts to unemployment insurance benefits, restrictions in the rate of growth of the Canada Assistance Plan transfers to the rich provinces for social assistance (the so-called cap on CAP), and cuts to subsidies to Crown corporations such as the CBC and VIA Rail.

7   *The Gallup Report*, Dec. 5, 1994, p. 2.

8   Reform Party of Canada, *Principles and Policies*, 1990, p. 15.

9   See Ken Battle (under the pseudonym Grattan Gray), "Social Policy by Stealth," *Policy Options*, vol. 11, no. 2, 1990, pp. 17-29, for more on the Mulroney government's clawbacks of income security benefits.

10 Reform Party of Canada, *Principles and Policies*, p. 20.

11 For a description of how guaranteed annual income schemes are intended to work and a summary of the various Canadian studies on the subject, see Patrick Grady, "Income Security Reform and the Concept of a Guaranteed Annual Income," Bryne B. Purchase, Research Director, Government and Competitiveness Research Series, *Redefining Social Security* (Kingston: School of Policy Studies, Queen's University, 1995), pp. 49-98.

12 *The Gallup Report*, April 24, 1993, p. 1.

13 *The Gallup Report*, April 24, 1993, p. 1.

14 Tom Courchene has argued that part of the reason for the depth of the early 1990s recession was a total lack of coordination between federal and provincial governments and the Bank of Canada on macroeconomic policy. In this instance we had the Mulroney government running big deficits during an economic boom, thereby fuelling inflation. At the same time, Ottawa was undertaking some major economic policy changes such as the Free Trade Agreement and the GST, causing significant transition problems for the private sector. Simultaneously, we had a big-spending government in Ontario at a time when the economy of Canada's largest province was overheating. Inflation thus became a big concern, and the Bank of Canada responded by jacking up interest rates in pursuit of price stability. We therefore had all of these authorities working at cross-purposes, which undoubtedly deepened and prolonged the recession.

This may illustrate one of the quintessential economic policy dilemmas in a federal state lacking formal macroeconomic coordination mechanisms between governments and the central bank.

15 See Thomas J. Courchene, "Zero Means Almost Nothing: Towards a Prefer-able Inflation and Macroeconomic Policy," *Queen's Quarterly*, vol. 97, no. 4 (winter 1990), pp. 543-61, which basically predicted that a policy-induced recession was in store for Canada.

16 See Courchene and Telmer, *From Heartland to North American Region State: The Social, Fiscal and Federal Evolution of Ontario* (Toronto: University of Toronto Press, 1998), regarding the negative impact of Ottawa's fiscal, trade, and monetary policies on the Ontario economy during the early 1990s.

17 *The Gallup Report*, Dec. 5, 1994, p. 2.

18 *The Gallup Report*, Dec. 5, 1994, p. 2.

19 *The Gallup Report*, July 31, 1995, p. 1.

20 *The Gallup Report*, Feb. 27, 1995, p. 1.

21 Reform Party of Canada, *A Fresh Start for Canadians*, 1996.

22 Murray Campbell, "Voters Willing to Give Up Tax Cuts," *Globe and Mail*, May 17, 1999, p. A5.

TWO: CANADA'S GEMINI TWINS

1 Between 1994 and 1998, Ontario's retail sales grew, on average, by 5 per-cent in nominal terms. Canada's sales expanded at a 4.5 percent clip per annum. In recent years the strongest growth and lowest unemployment in Canada have been in Saskatchewan, where the NDP government actually raised taxes.

2 Angus Reid, "Ontario: Into the Election Window."

THREE: MUDDLING THROUGH WITH JEAN CHRÉTIEN'S LIBERALS

1 William Walker, "Which Way Will Chrétien Turn?" *Toronto Star*, March 13, 1999.

2 The Liberal Party of Canada, *Creating Opportunity: The Liberal Plan for Canada* (Ottawa: The Liberal Party of Canada, 1993).

3 Edward Greenspon and Anthony Wilson-Smith, *Double Vision: The Inside*

Story of the Liberals in Power (Toronto: Doubleday Canada, 1996).

4   Government of Canada, *A New Framework for Economic Policy* (known as the Purple Book) (Ottawa: Department of Finance, October 1994), p. 73.

5   Government of Canada, *The Budget Plan 1994* (Ottawa: Department of Finance, Feb. 1994), p. 1.

6   The world-renowned Canadian-born economist Robert Mundell recently stated that the British-born and Oxford-educated Crow simply did not have a sophisticated understanding of the Canadian economy, and especially of the variations in economic structure throughout Canada, and that this may partly explain his heavy-handed approach to monetary policy.

7   For a good analysis of the Program Review exercise, see Gilles Pacquet and Robert Shepherd, "The Program Review Process: A Deconstruction," Gene Swimmer, ed., *How Ottawa Spends 1996-97: Life Under the Knife* (Ottawa: Carleton University Press, 1996).

8   For analysis of the Axworthy Social Policy Review, see Keith Banting and Ken Battle, eds., *A New Social Vision for Canada: Perspectives on the Federal Discussion Paper on Social Security Reform* (Kingston: School of Policy Studies and Caledon Institute of Social Policy, 1994).

9   Government of Canada, *Improving Social Security in Canada* (Ottawa: Human Resources Development Canada, Oct. 5, 1994). Also known as the Green Paper.

10   Purple Book, pp. 14-15.

11   Purple Book, p. 84.

12   Authors' conversation with Peter Nicholson, June 1998.

13   The Red Book spending restraint measures were limited to politically innocuous things such as cancellation of the Mulroney government's plan to purchase expensive helicopters for the military, general cuts in defence spending, and reductions in the size and budget of Cabinet ministers' offices and the Prime Minister's Office. Red Book, p. 20.

14   Greenspon, Wilson-Smith, *Double Vision*, p. 196.

15   Government of Canada, *Budget Plan 1995* (Ottawa: Department of Finance, Feb. 27, 1995), p. 6.

16   Some claim that DIAND's budget was spared in 1994-95 because it had already undergone its own program review exercise under the Tories a

few years earlier and in light of the federal government's fiduciary responsibility for on-reserve Aboriginals. Equalization was left untouched due in part to national unity considerations; Quebec is the largest beneficiary of this program.

17 For a thorough analysis of the CHST, see Thomas J. Courchene, *Redistributing Power and Money: A Guide to the Canada Health and Social Transfer* (Toronto: C.D. Howe Institute, 1995).

18 Don Mazankowski was apparently presented with a CHST-like block fund option by his officials while he was the Tory finance minister, but rejected it as too radical.

19 Government of Canada, *The Budget Plan 1996* (Ottawa: Department of Finance, March 6, 1996), p. 64.

20 See Government of Canada, *The Budget Plan, 1999* (Ottawa: Department of Finance, Feb. 16, 1999), for the details of these spending initiatives.

21 See, for example, John Richards, *Retooling the Welfare State* (Toronto: C.D. Howe Institute, 1997). Richards quotes the National Forum on Health as follows: "Without exception, all [recent provincial] reviews have concluded that the health care system needs better management, not more money. We believe this to be true today, even though health care budgets have been frozen or reduced in many jurisdictions over the last few years" (p. 126). The *Globe and Mail* has also made this argument. See "Money Won't Cure What Ails Medicare," *Globe and Mail*, Feb. 15, 1999, p. A12. So have others such as economist Douglas Angus in "Better Management, Not More Cash, Prescribed for Canadian Health Care System," *Canadian Business Economics*, vol. 7, no. 1 (Feb. 1999), pp. 15-20, and Michael Strofolino, President and CEO of the Hospital for Sick Children, in "A Priority for Our Health Care: More Nurses," *Globe and Mail*, Feb. 23, 1999, p. A17.

22 Calculated from J. Harvey Perry, *A Fiscal History of Canada: The Post War Years* (Toronto: Canadian Tax Foundation, 1989).

23 See, for example, John McCallum, "The Non-neoconservative Case for Lower Income Taxes," *National Post*, March 23, 1999, p. C7, in which McCallum, a respected bank economist, suggests $10 billion surpluses will become commonplace.

24 Through its reforms of federal-provincial transfers and unemployment insurance, Ottawa has insulated itself from sudden and unforeseen increases in these expenses such as have been common in the past. Nevertheless, fiscal risk from a recession remains worrying, especially if a government caves in to political pressure to make these programs too generous again.

Four: Present at the Creation: Keynes in the Modern World

1 Canada, Dominion-Provincial Conference on Reconstruction, *Proposals of the Government of Canada* (Ottawa, King's Printer, 1945).

2 J.L. Granatstein, *The Ottawa Men: The Civil Service Mandarins, 1935-1957* (Toronto: University of Toronto Press, 1982), p. 257.

3 Robert Bryce, *Maturing in Hard Times: Canada's Department of Finance Through the Great Depression* (Kingston and Montreal: McGill-Queen's University Press, 1986), p. ix.

4 Robert Skidelsky, *John Maynard Keynes: Economist as Saviour* (London: Penguin, 1992), p .5.

5 Ian Drummond, "Economic History and Canadian Economic Performance Since the Second World War," John Sargent, Research Coordinator, *Postwar Macroeconomic Developments*, Royal Commission on the Economic Union and Development Prospects for Canada ("MacDonald Commission") (Toronto: University of Toronto Press, 1985), p. 11.

6 Bryce, *Maturing in Hard Times*, p. 46.

7 Bryce, *Maturing in Hard Times*, p. 113.

8 Keynes visited Roosevelt in Washington during the 1930s to impress his ideas upon him, and while unconvinced at first, Roosevelt eventually came to believe in the Keynesian gospel.

9 Charles Dunning, *House of Commons Debates*, April 25, 1939, p. 3446.

10 Government of Canada, *Employment and Income* (Ottawa: King's Printer, 1945).

11 Government of Canada, *Employment and Income*, p. 21.

12 Perry, *A Fiscal History of Canada*, p. 151.

13 For more on the reasons for the development of the welfare state in Canada, see Keith G. Banting, *The Welfare State and Canadian Federal-*

ism (Kingston and Montreal: McGill-Queen's University Press, 1982).

14   Bernard Fortin, "Income Security in Canada," Francois Vaillancourt, Research Coordinator, *Income Distribution and Economic Security in Canada*, Royal Commission on the Economic Union and Development Prospects for Canada (Toronto: University of Toronto Press, 1985), p. 158, table 4-1.

15   David A. Dodge, "Reflections on the Role of Fiscal Policy: The Doug Purvis Memorial Lecture," *Canadian Public Policy*, vol. 24, no. 3, 1998, p. 277, table 1.

16   Paul Krugman, *Peddling Prosperity: Economic Sense and Nonsense in the Age of Diminished Expectations* (New York: W.W. Norton, 1994), p. 15.

17   Perry, *A Fiscal History of Canada*, p. 695, table 23.2.

18   Perry, *A Fiscal History of Canada*, p. 95.

19   Douglas D. Purvis and Constance Smith, "Fiscal Policy in Canada, 1963-84," John Sargent, Research Coordinator, *Fiscal and Monetary Policy*, Royal Commission on the Economic Union and Development Prospects for Canada (Toronto: University of Toronto Press, 1985), p. 12, table 1-6.

FIVE: MONETARISTS AS BOMB THROWERS

1   Christine McCall-Newman, *Grits: An Intimate Portrait of the Liberal Party* (Toronto: Macmillan of Canada, 1982), p. 227.

2   Perry, *A Fiscal History of Canada*, p. 9.

3   This figure is calculated by adding two percentage points to the previous year's inflation rate. The two-percentage point figure was the average annual increase of prices between 1971 and 1975.

4   John Saywell, ed., *Canadian Annual Review of Politics and Public Affairs*, 1976 (Toronto: University of Toronto Press, 1977), p. 338.

5   Saywell, ed., *Canadian Annual Review of Politics and Public Affairs*, 1976, p. 348.

6   Robert M. Campbell, *The Full Employment Objective in Canada, 1945-85* (Ottawa: The Economic Council of Canada, 1991), p. 11.

7   Saywell, ed., *Canadian Annual Review of Politics and Public Affairs*, 1976, p. 383.

8   "In a speech to University of California at Berkeley undergraduates, Fisher

railed against government intervention to increase employment." Joel Glenn Brenner, *The Emperors of Chocolate* (New York: Random House, 1999), p. 55.

9   Todd Buchholz, *New Ideas from Dead Economists* (New York: Plume Publishing, 1989), p. 226.

10 Preamble to the Bank of Canada Act.

11 Michael Parkin, *Modern Macroeconomics* (Toronto: Prentice Hall Canada, 1982), p. 515.

12 Perry, *A Fiscal History of Canada*, p. 10.

13 Peter Howitt, *Monetary Policy in Transition: A Study of Bank of Canada Policy, 1982-85* (Toronto: C.D. Howe Institute, 1986), p. 76.

14 Adapted from Howitt, *Monetary Policy in Transition*, pp. 64, 77.

15 David Laidler and William Robson, *The Great Canadian Disinflation* (Toronto: C.D. Howe Institute, 1993), p. 79.

16 Laidler and Robson, *The Great Canadian Disinflation*, p. 120.

17 Linda McQuaig, *The Cult of Impotence* (Toronto: Penguin Books Canada, 1998), p. 133.

Six: The Strange World of Rational Expectations

1   David Fettig, ed., "Time to Learn New Things," *The Region*, vol. 9, no. 4, Dec. 1995, p. 45.

2   Fettig, ed., "Time to Learn New Things."

3   Rupert Pennant-Rea and Clive Crook, *The Economist Economics* (London: Penguin Books, 1988), p. 160.

4   Buchholz, *New Ideas from Dead Economists*, p. 266.

5   Clarence Nelson, "Rational Expectations — Fresh Ideas That Challenge Some Established Views of Policy Making," 1977 Annual Report of the Federal Reserve Bank of Minneapolis, p. 1.

6   Carl Walsh, "Nobel Views on Inflation and Unemployment," *Federal Reserve Bank of San Francisco Economic Letter*, no. 97-01, Jan. 10, 1997.

7   McQuaig, *The Cult of Impotence*, p. 40.

8   This situation assumes that the government also boosts available social assistance and employment insurance payments to reflect higher inflation. If not, it might pay people to work even if they are not getting more

money after subtracting inflation. That's because they are losing money, in real terms, by not working and relying solely upon inflation-reduced government handouts.

9   Buchholz, *New Ideas from Dead Economists*, p. 273.

10 Nelson, "Rational Expectations — Fresh Ideas That Challenge Some Established Views of Policy Making," p. 8.

11 This example comes from the lecture notes of Roger Ashton McCain, professor of economics, Drexel University.

12 Authors' conversation with Professor McCain.

13 "Journey Beyond the Stars," *The Economist*, Dec. 19, 1998, p. 108.

14 Interview with Thomas Sargent, *The Region*, vol. 3, no. 3, Dec. 1998, p. 14.

SEVEN: GROWING INTO PROSPERITY

1   Bernard Wysocki Jr., "Wealth of Notions," *Wall Street Journal*, Jan. 21, 1997.

2   Gregory Mankiw, "The Reincarnation of Keynesian Economics," *European Economic Review* (1992) 36, as reprinted in Brian Snowden and Howard Vane, eds., *A Macroeconomics Reader* (London: Routledge, 1997), p. 445.

3   Lucas has written one of the more important articles on the subject, "On the Mechanics of Economic Development," *Journal of Monetary Economics* (July 22, 1988), pp. 3-42.

4   Milton Friedman and Rose Friedman, *Free to Choose* (New York: Harcourt, Brace, Jovanovitch, 1980), p. 206.

5   Snowden and Vane, *A Macroeconomics Reader*, p. 577.

6   Jeffrey Frankel, "Why Economies Grow the Way They Do," *Canadian Business Economics*, vol. 6, no. 3 (Sept. 1998), p. 3.

7   Paul Romer, "The Origins of Endogenous Growth" *Journal of Economic Perspectives*, vol. 8, no. 1 (Winter 1994), p. 4. Others, such as Moses Abramovitz, have made similar observations. In his case, Abramovitz compared the relative productivity of the U.S. and fifteen other countries over a period of 107 years. He found that the 23 percentage point advantage that the U.S. enjoyed in 1870 had actually increased to 25 percentage points by 1979. Moses Abramovitz, "Catching Up, Forging Ahead and Falling Behind," in Snowden and Vane, *A Macroeconomics Reader*, pp. 582-603.

8   Paul Romer, "Increasing Returns and Long-Run Growth," *Journal of*

Political Economy, vol. 94, no. 5, 1986, p. 1003.

9   Frankel, "Why Economies Grow the Way They Do," p. 3.

10   Barry McKenna, "Canada's Ranking Slips in Ability to Innovate," *Globe and Mail,* March 12, 1999, p. B3.

EIGHT: A DIMINUTIVE GALBRAITH FOR THE 1990S

1   Robert B. Reich, *The Work of Nations* (New York: Vintage Books, 1992), p. 109.

2   *Economist,* "Innovation in Industry," Feb. 20, 1999, p. 28.

3   For more on Galbraith's career and thinking, see John Kenneth Galbraith, *A Life in Our Times* (Boston: Houghton Mifflin, 1981).

4   Introduction of John Kenneth Galbraith by Robert Pritchard, Keith Davey Lecture, Victoria University, University of Toronto, Jan. 7, 1997.

5   Paul Krugman, *Peddling Prosperity: Economic Sense and Nonsense in the Age of Diminished Expectations* (New York: W.W. Norton, 1994).

6   For more on Reich's efforts to implement his ideas in the Clinton administration, see Robert B. Reich, *Locked in the Cabinet* (New York: Alfred A. Knopf, 1997).

7   Reich, *The Work of Nations,* p.113.

8   Reich, *The Work of Nations,* p. 98.

9   Reich, *The Work of Nations,* pp. 184, 196.

10   Reich, *The Work of Nations,* p. 154.

11   See Krugman, *Peddling Prosperity,* for such a criticism.

12   Krugman attributes the origin of Reich's international-trade-human-capital theory to the early writings on "factor price equalization" of the Nobel laureate Paul Samuelson; *Peddling Prosperity,* p. 146.

13   The Canadian literature on this subject is surveyed by W. Craig Riddell in "Human Capital Formation in Canada: Recent Developments and Policy Responses," Keith G. Banting and Charles Beach, eds., *Labour Market Polarization and Social Policy Reform* (Kingston: School of Policy Studies, Queen's University, 1995) pp. 126-72.

14   Economic Council of Canada, *Employment in the Service Economy* (Ottawa: Minister of Supply and Services, 1991).

15   Government of Canada, *The Budget Plan 1999* (Ottawa: Department of

Finance, Feb. 16, 1999), p. 116, chart 5.3.

16 Budget 1999, pp. 117, 104.

17 Lars Osberg, Fred Wien, and Jan Grude, *Vanishing Jobs: Canada's Changing Workplaces* (Toronto: James Lorimer, 1995), p. 160.

18 One reason why the education premium was greater in the U.S. than in Canada in the 1980s may be that Canada had a proportionately greater supply of university and college graduates than the U.S., which is partly attributable to our more financially accessible system of PSE. See René Morisette, John Myles, and Garnett Picot, "Earnings Polarization in Canada, 1969-91," Keith G. Banting and Charles M. Beach, eds., *Labour Market Polarization and Social Policy Reform* (Kingston: School of Policy Studies, Queen's University, 1995), p. 46.

19 Osberg, Wien, and Grude, *Vanishing Jobs*, pp. 158, 160.

20 Government of Canada, *Budget Plan* 1995 (Ottawa: Department of Finance, Feb. 27, 1995), p. 51, table 4.4.

21 Riddell, "Human Capital Formation in Canada," p. 145.

22 Tom Kent, *Social Policy 2000: An Agenda* (Ottawa: Caledon Institute of Social Policy, Jan. 1999), p. 21.

23 Earnscliffe Research and Communications, *Presentation to the Department of Finance: Pre-Budget Survey* (Ottawa: Feb. 1999).

NINE: PUSHING POLICIES FOR THE NEXT CENTURY

1 Gordon Betcherman, Kathryn McMullen, and Katie Davidson, *Training for the New Economy* (Ottawa: Canada Policy Research Networks, 1998), p. 55.

2 Speech by Charles Sirois, chairman and chief executive officer, Teleglobe Inc., given to the Canadian Club of Montreal, Feb. 22, 1998.

3 An example of the outmoded approach of Ottawa's Atlantic Canada regional development agency, known as ACOA, occurred recently when a firm applied for a business loan and was rejected on the grounds that it was a service business: ACOA claimed they only supported manufacturing industries. Having said that, ACOA saw fit to provide money to the lucrative 1998 Skins Golf Tournament in PEI.

4 Axworthy floated the ICR idea when he was minister of human resources

development in Government of Canada, *Improving Social Security in Canada* (Ottawa: Department of Human Resources Development, 1994).

5   Warren Clark, "Paying off Student Loans," *Statistics Canada: Perspectives on Labour and Income*, vol. 11, no. 1 (Spring 1999), p. 28.

6   Economist Lars Osberg, one of the few heretics, puts it this way: "Some of the expensive types of education (medicine, law) produce graduates whose incomes are sufficiently high that ICR could cover the costs, but other expensive programs (science PhDs) produce graduates whose lifetime earnings are not high. Could we expect continued enrolment in post-graduate science programs if such were the case?" Lars Osberg, "Jobs and Growth: the Missing Link," Keith Banting and Ken Battle, eds., *A New Social Vision for Canada: Perspectives on the Federal Discussion Paper on Social Security Reform* (Kingston: School of Policy Studies, Queen's University, 1994), p. 64.

7   Thomas J. Courchene, "Potholes in the Road to Reform," Banting and Battle, eds., *A New Social Vision for Canada*, p. 22, fn. 4.

8   Tom Kent, *Social Policy 2000: An Agenda* (Ottawa: Caledon Institute of Social Policy, 1999).

9   There is nothing in the Social Union Framework Agreement that precludes the federal government from establishing a new program of financial transfers to individuals, except a condition to consult with the provinces in advance. See Government of Canada, *Collaborative Use of the Spending Power for Intergovernmental Transfers: The Race to the Top Model* (Ottawa: Feb. 5, 1999) and Government of Canada, *A Framework to Improve the Social Union for Canadians* (Ottawa: Feb. 4, 1999).

10 Before the advent of the CHST, Courchene advocated converting the EPF-PSE cash transfer into a voucher system for students. See Courchene, "Potholes on the Road to Reform."

11 A recent study by the Canadian Labour Force Development Board concludes that the provinces that have signed labour market development agreements with Ottawa lack the administrative and policy infrastructure to assume these responsibilities and are making a mess of labour market policy in their jurisdictions. See Canadian Labour Force Development

Board, *State of Labour Market Programs and Services in Canada* (Ottawa: Dec. 1998).

12 Raymond Koskie's correspondence to and conversations with the authors, Jan. 1999.

13 Kent, *Social Policy 2000*, p. 20.

INDEX